How to Study

3rd Edition

By
Ron Fry

CAREER PRESS
180 Fifth Avenue
P.O. Box 34
Hawthorne, NJ 07507
1-800-CAREER-1
201-427-0229 (outside U.S.)
FAX: 201-427-2037

Copyright © 1994 by Ron Fry

HOW TO STUDY (3RD ED.)
ISBN 1-56414-075-X, $9.95
Cover design by A Good Thing, Inc.
Printed in the U.S.A. by Book-mart Press

To order this title by mail, please include price as noted above, $2.50 handling per order, and $1.00 for each book ordered. Send to: Career Press, Inc., 180 Fifth Ave., P.O. Box 34, Hawthorne, NJ 07507.

Or call toll-free 1-800-CAREER-1 (Canada: 201-427-0229) to order using VISA or MasterCard, or for further information on books from Career Press.

Library of Congress Cataloging-in-Publication Data

Fry, Ronald W.
    How to study / by Ron Fry. -- 3rd ed.
      p.   cm.
    Includes index.
    ISBN 1-56414-075-X
    1. Study skills. I. Title.
LB1049.F74   1994
371.3'028'12--dc20
                                           94-5487
                                             CIP

Ron Fry's

HOW TO STUDY
PROGRAM

How to Study, 3rd Ed. (ISBN 1-56414-075-X, 224 pp., $9.95)

"Ace" Any Test, 2nd Ed. (ISBN 1-56414-079-2, 128 pp., $6.95)

Improve Your Memory, 2nd Ed. (ISBN 1-56414-080-6, 128 pp., $6.95)

Improve Your Reading, 2nd Ed. (ISBN 1-56414-077-6, 128 pp., $6.95)

Manage Your Time, 2nd Ed. (ISBN 1-56414-078-4, 128 pp., $6.95)

Take Notes, 2nd Ed. (ISBN 1-56414-076-8, 128 pp., $6.95)

Write Papers, 2nd Ed. (ISBN 1-56414-081-4, 128 pp., $6.95)

Available individually at your favorite bookstore or as a set by calling 1-800-CAREER-1.

STUDY SMARTER, NOT HARDER!

Ron Fry's **HOW TO STUDY** ***Program,*** the best-selling and most acclaimed study series of all time, has sold more than 1,000,000 copies in four years. It is used in colleges, high schools and junior highs and by parents and students throughout the world. And Ron has appeared on hundreds of radio and TV shows and countless newspaper and magazine articles and profiles again and again to trumpet his message: Study Smarter, Not Harder!

Here are just a few of the things reviewers have said about ***Ron Fry's*** **HOW TO STUDY** ***Program:***

"These books belong in every secondary library and perhaps in every English classroom. **Highly recommended.**"
— *Library Materials Guide*, Christian Schools International

How to Study

"Fry's **lively style of writing** makes the book **very useful**."
— *Library Journal*

"Fry has an **appealing, down-to-earth style** that makes this text **accessible and practical**. A regular classroom teacher could extract pertinent lessons to prepare all students to be more successful scholars. The Series would also be appropriate for self-study by college students."
— *Intervention* magazine

"...**approachable, chatty and interactive.** Fry speaks directly to the reader in an **encouraging and sympathetic** fashion it will benefit students from high school age on up."
— *Kliatt Young Adult Paperback Guide*

"...I really liked *How to Study*. **A great gift** for any student."
— *Bookviews*

"**Wow! This guy makes sense, he's funny, and he is easy to read.** I got the feeling this approach might even work for me!"
— Virginia Meldrum, owner of the Owl's Tree bookstore

"This series **could be useful in resource rooms, in a regular classroom setting or as a self-study guide**."
— Learning Disabilities Association of Canada

Table of

CONTENTS

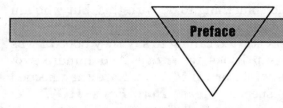

I first wrote **How to Study** in 1988, convinced that schools were doing a lousy job of teaching kids how to study—synonymous, to me, with teaching them how to *learn*—and that no one was picking up the slack. (I was also convinced—and still am—that most kids wanted *desperately* to learn but would, without some help, find it easier to fail. And failure, once welcomed, is a very nasty habit to break.)

Published in 1989, most bookstores wedged one or two copies of **Study** in between the hundreds of phone book-sized test prep volumes. Career Press wasn't a big enough publisher to convince the "chains"—Waldenbooks, Barnes & Noble, B. Dalton—to stock it in any quantity or rich enough to spend any money promoting it.

Nevertheless, tens of thousands of people who obviously needed **How to Study** ferreted out copies wherever they lurked and bought them. In 1990, the chains—who *are* smart enough to at least spot a winner the *second* time around—bought 6-copy "prepacks" and gave the book a little more prominence. (Meaning you didn't have to get a hernia removing other books to find a copy of **Study**.) Career Press sent me around the country to appear on radio and TV, including CNN. And hundreds of newspapers and magazines noticed what we were doing and started writing about **How to Study**. (The fact that test scores had declined for the hundred-fortieth year in a row or so probably had something to do with this, but who am I to quibble with the attention?)

In 1991, *booksellers* started calling to say they hoped I was planning some follow-up books to **Study**. And hundreds of parents and students wrote or called to indicate they needed more help in some specific areas. **Ron Fry's HOW TO STUDY *Program*** was born, featuring a second edition of **Study** and four new books—*Improve Your Reading, Manage Your Time, Take Notes and Write Papers*—that delved even deeper into critical study skills. That year I spent more time on the phone doing radio shows than I did, I think, with my wife and 2-year-old daughter.

In 1992, I added two more volumes—***"Ace" Any Test*** and ***Improve Your Memory***, both of which were pretty much written in response to readers' letters. The latter was, as far as I was concerned, a natural extension of ***Improve Your Reading***, which had dealt primarily with the reading process and only peripherally with ways to increase comprehension. ***Memory*** also delved into problems people faced remembering names, faces, dates, math formulas and a host of others.

Test, on the other hand, was a book I really didn't want to write, since I was (and am) convinced that we are a society tested to death, usually without any clear understanding of what's being tested—or what the results are supposed to mean. Since so many people think learning to study is almost exclusively learning to "take tests," I was also afraid I would undermine my message: Learning how to take a test is a *very* small part of learning how to study. Nevertheless, acknowledging that standardized testing is here to stay meant at least doing my bit to help students do the best they could on the alphabets (SAT, PSAT, ACT, etc., etc., etc.)

Surprisingly, ***Memory*** and ***Test*** quickly became the second- and third-biggest sellers of the seven books in the series, beaten only by ***How to Study***. Evidently, my readers knew darned well what they were requesting.

By the way, in both 1992 and 1993, I added mightily to my Frequent Flyer accounts while talking to people nationwide about studying. I wound up visiting 50 cities, some twice, and appearing on more TV and radio shows than are listed in your daily newspaper.

The result of all this travel was twofold: First, sales of all seven books have skyrocketed, in part because of the chance I've been given to talk about them on so many shows and in so many newspapers and magazines. Second, I got to meet and talk with tens of thousands of students and parents, so many of whom confirmed the ongoing need for these books *because very little has changed since I first wrote* **How to Study** *some six years ago.*

Test scores of every kind are lower today than they were then. More and more students are dropping out or, if they *do* manage to graduate high school, are finding they are not equipped to do *any*-thing, whether they're hoping to go to college or trying to land a job. And more and more parents are frustrated by their children's inability to learn and their schools' seeming inability to teach.

With so much new feedback, it was time to revise all seven books, all of which are being published in time for "back to school" in 1994. In every book, I've included additional topics and expanded on others. I've changed some examples, simplified some, eliminated some. I've rewritten sentences, paragraphs or entire sections that students seemed to be struggling with. Most importantly, I've tried to reflect my new understanding of just who is reading these books—"traditional" students, their parents *and* nontraditional (i.e. older, perhaps much older) students, many of those self-same parents—and write in such a way to include all three audiences.

I hope after reading these books you'll agree I've succeeded.

I'm sure after reading these books that *you'll* succeed.

Ron Fry

May, 1994

HOW TO USE THIS BOOK

What one knows is, in youth, of little moment;
they know enough who know how to learn.
— Henry Adams

Learning how to study *is* learning how to *learn*. And that is, to me, the greatest gift you can ever give yourself.

Having stated that so boldly, I suspect I still have to convince some of you that spending any time trying to master this stuff—studying, learning, reading, note-taking, writing, whatever you call it—is worth your while.

Believe it or not, there are some terrific reasons why you *should* learn how to study, why you *must* learn how to study. But before I start convincing you that developing proper study skills really *is* important and why, let's figure out exactly what we mean by "study skills" so we're all on the same wavelength.

10

Yes, **How to Study** includes hints, advice and techniques for taking notes in class, while you're reading your textbooks, even in the library. And how to prepare for tests. And how to organize your study schedule to get the best results in the shortest amount of time. But that's the *last* half of the book. There are essential skills you may think don't even have anything to do with studying, and important steps you need to take right from the start.

Here's where to start

> Learn as though you would never be able to
> master it; hold it as if you would be in fear of
> losing it.
> — Confucius

Developing great study habits is like a race between you and all your friends around a track. Before you can declare a winner, you have to agree on where the finish line is. In other words, how do you measure your ability to use these skills? What's good? What's poor?

But you can't even start the race until you know where the *starting* line is—especially if it's drawn at a different spot for each of you!

Chapter 1 starts by explaining each study skill and clarifying how each can and should function in your life. Then you have the chance to find your own starting line.

This first chapter is the most important, because your own honest assessment of how well you have already mastered basic study habits will set the tone for your entire approach to the guidelines you will find throughout this book.

In Chapter 2, you'll learn the importance of where, how and when you study and start building the study environment that's perfectly right for *you*. Why is this important? If you've spent three hours reading **Great Expectations** with The Lemonheads shaking the walls, it's not surprising that you're still on page 3! Reading and understanding Mr. Dickens might have little to do with increasing your reading comprehension, rescheduling your time or changing books—and a lot more to do with just turning down the volume.

There is no magic elixir in the study habit regimen. If math and science are not your strong suits, memorizing **How to Study** will not transform you into a Nobel Prize-winning physicist. Nobody is great at *every*thing, but everybody is great at *some*thing. So you'll also get a chance to rate the subjects you like and dislike, plus those classes you do best and worst in. You'll find in later chapters that applying yourself to the subjects in which you need the most work is a simple, logical and successful way to alter your current habits without necessarily studying harder or longer.

Chapter 2 also introduces some of the "intangibles" in the study equation: your home environment, attitude, motivation, etc. If you are dedicated to the study discipline and motivated to achieve certain goals, all the other factors that affect your study habits will fall more naturally into place. A belief in the study ethic is one of the keys to success.

Finally, some generalities about the study process—learning to "read" teachers, developing mentors, dealing with perfectionism, the importance of flexibility—will help you start off right.

Reading and comprehension

Chapter 3 introduces the skills basic to any study process: reading and comprehension. No matter how well you learn to take notes, how familiar you become with your library, how doggedly you study for tests, if you are reading poorly (or not enough) and not understanding what you read, life will be difficult.

Becoming a good reader is a skill, one usually acquired early in life. If it's a skill you haven't acquired yet, now is the time!

Effective reading is a combination of comprehension and retention. Chapter 3 will help you find the proper balance of these elements. It will also help you work on concentration—the ability to focus on the printed page to the exclusion of all else, a skill all superior readers have.

Learning how to remember more of what you read is more important than reading faster. Chapter 3 also points out how your ability to recall ideas, facts and figures can be significantly increased (both quantitatively and qualitatively) with the right kind of practice.

Making up for lost time

To see a significant change in your life, many of you will not need to study *harder,* just *smarter.* Which means making better use of your study time—spending the same two or three or four hours but accomplishing twice or thrice or four times what you do now. Chapter 4 introduces the simplest and easiest-to-use organizational and time management tools you'll ever find, powerful ways to make sure you are always on track, including guidelines to develop both short-term and long-term calendars.

Go to the head of the class

In Chapter 5, I talk about the one experience we all have in common, no matter how old we are—the classroom. I'll help you take better notes, encourage your active participation in class discussions—including pointers on how to overcome the more natural tendency to hide behind the potted plant in the back of the room—and get a lot more out of lectures.

Learning your library

Chapter 6 introduces you to the single most important resource in your study career—your library. Whether you live in a small town, where library volumes are counted in the thousands and "current" might mean 5-years old, or a large city, where the library stacks kiss the sky and contain answers you don't even have questions for yet, learning how to take advantage of this great collection of knowledge is very important.

You'll learn about the kinds of books, periodicals, newspapers, magazines, computer software, video and audio tapes and other reference materials available to you and suggestions for how to find and use them, including an explanation of the Dewey Decimal Classification and Library of Congress Systems.

So you're not the next Hemingway

No matter how confident you are in your writing ability, I doubt you cheer when papers are assigned. Get used to it. In college, term papers are a regular part of virtually every class you take. And don't think graduation ends the chore. You'll be writing "papers" of some kind—business letters, presentations, proposals, long memos—in almost any career you choose. And your ability to clearly and concisely express your views and communicate facts, figures and ideas will strongly influence how fast you advance in your chosen career.

I'm convinced that too many of you place the emphasis in "writing papers" on the word "writing." In Chapter 7, I'll introduce you to a remarkably easy way to gather research, take notes and organize your information. By breaking down any paper, no matter how complex, into easy-to-follow steps, I think you'll find you create papers infinitely better than before—even if you're still no threat to Hemingway (or anybody else) when it comes to writing.

Use a No. 2 pencil

Chapter 8 covers the do's and don'ts of test preparation, including the differences between studying for weekly quizzes, mid-terms and final examinations, why last-minute cramming doesn't work (but how to do it if you have no other choice—shame!), studying for and taking different types of tests (multiple choice, true-false, essay, open book, etc.), how to increase your guessing scores, even which questions to answer first and which to leave for last.

No senior citizen discounts

A man must always study, but he must not always go to school.
— Montaigne

You will always have to study. Whether you want to be an engineer, doctor, construction worker, artist, dancer, auto mechanic or businessman, be prepared to study. Never have the demands of our society been so great and the burdens on individuals so weighty. And don't believe that when you finally leave school—whether as a dropout or with a Ph.D.—that your days in the classroom and library are over. You will encounter new classrooms throughout your lifetime.

Even if we discount the intangible benefits of education—a more complete and fulfilling life, access to more and more interesting people, places and things, etc.—the practical rewards of education can be measured in very real dollars and cents terms: The more you learn, the more you earn.

Land any but the most menial job and chances are there will be a training program. The more complicated the job—whether it's primarily manual or professional—the faster and more often you will find yourself back in the classroom. Some training programs at major corporations last for months.

Yes, you'll be back in school, whatever your age, and it's too late to learn how to study now!

Taking notes? Watch what happens during that first sales meeting when 40 new products are flashed on the screen, one right after the other. You'd better be ready to quickly and accurately write down what you need to know to go out and explain them to your prospective customers.

Asking your boss to repeat himself doesn't wash.

How to Study

Job promotion? Even if your lack of advanced schooling forced you to start at a clerical or blue-collar job, your natural talents might send you up the ladder of success. When that promotion to a white-collar job or even a management position does come, you'll be happy to know your company is paying all your expenses for that highly touted, three-day management training seminar. Yes, it's intense.

Yes, you'd better be ready to learn and assimilate the material quickly. And yes, you're back in school again!

Through all stages of life, opportunities to acquire new knowledge and expand your horizons will constantly present themselves. Will you be ready to take advantage of all those wonderful opportunities?

How smart do *you* study?

Will this book really help you? Yes, it really will. **How to Study** is the most comprehensive study guide ever written—a fundamental, step-by-step approach that *you* can follow to develop and sharpen your study skills.

If you're struggling through college or graduate school, here's your life raft.

If you're a high school student planning to attend college, hone your study skills *now*.

If you're heading for trade school, planning to dance, write, paint, etc., not considering college, even if you're ready to drop out of high school at the earliest possible instant, you need **How to Study**.

And if you're an adult returning to the classroom after a lengthy absence, there is no substitute for the tips and techniques you will learn in this helpful collection of study procedures.

What if you're a really poor student? So what?

How smart you are is not the point. *What counts is how smart you study.*

With the possible exception of those 2 percent of you who qualify as "gifted," the effective study habits *How to Study* teaches will help students of any age:

If your grades are average to good, you will see a definite difference. If you are on the borderline of the pass/fail range, you will benefit considerably. If good study habits are in place but rusty as a result of years away from the classroom, *How to Study* is the perfect refresher for you.

And if you *are* one of those "2 percent gifted," I *still* think you'll find some helpful techniques in these pages.

Who is this book *really* for?

While I originally wrote *How to Study* for high school students, I've discovered over the years that I could probably count on a couple of hands the number of such students who actually bought a copy of the book. Oh, students do indeed buy *How to Study*, but they're either already in college (which says wonderful things about the preparation they got in high school), in junior high (which says something much more positive about their motivation and, probably, eventual success) or returning to college (about whom more later).

The surprise was that so many of the people buying *How to Study* (and writing me reams of letters along the way) were adults. Yes, a number of them were returning to school and saw *How to Study* as a great refresher. And some were long out of school but had figured out that if they could learn *now* the study skills their teachers never taught them, they'd do better in their careers.

All too many were parents who had the same lament: "How do I get Johnny (Janie) to read (study, do better on tests, remember more, get better grades, etc.)?"

So I want to briefly take the time to address every one of the audiences for this book and discuss some of the factors particular to each of you.

17

How to Study

If you're a high school student

You should be particularly comfortable with the format of the book—its relatively short sentences and paragraphs, occasionally humorous (hopefully) headings and subheadings—and the language used. I wrote it with you in mind!

But you should also be *un*comfortable with the fact that you're already in the middle of your school years—the period that will drastically affect, one way or the other, all the *rest* of your school years—*and you still don't know how to study!* Don't lose another minute. Make learning how to study and mastering *all* of the study skills in this book your *absolute priority*.

If you're a junior high school student

Congratulations! You are trying to learn how to study at *precisely* the right time. Sixth, seventh and eighth grades—before that sometimes cosmic leap to high school—is without a doubt the period in which all these study skills should be mastered, since doing so will make high school not just easier but a far more positive and successful experience. Although written for high school-level readers, if you're serious enough about studying to be reading this book, I doubt you'll have trouble with the concepts or the language.

If you're a traditional college student...

...somewhere in the 18 to 25 age range, I hope you are tackling one or two of the study skills you failed to master in high school (in which case I highly recommend you also study the appropriate title(s) of the other six books in my **HOW TO STUDY** *Program—"Ace" Any Test"*, *Improve Your Memory, Improve Your Reading, Manage Your Time, Take Notes* and *Write Papers*). Otherwise, I can't see how you're ever going to succeed in college (then again, I can't conceive of how you managed to get *into* college). If you are starting from

18

scratch, my advice is the same as to the high school students reading this book: Drop everything and make it your number one priority. Do not pass Go. Do not order pizza.

If you're the parent of a student of any age

You must be convinced of one incontestable fact: It is highly unlikely that your child's school is doing anything to teach him or her how to study. Yes, of course they should. Yes, I know that's what you thought you paid taxes for. Yes, yes, yes. But, but, but—believe me, *they're not doing it*.

How do I know? For one thing, in thousands of interviews on radio, TV and in the print media, my publisher has allowed me to make the same offer: They will give any teacher or school administrator wishing to use any or all of the books in my **HOW TO STUDY** *Program* one *free* book for every one they purchase. That's right, buy 10, get 10 free. Buy 100, get 100 free.

There are three teachers out there—all three spending *their own money*, mind you—who have taken me up on that offer. Says something about priorities, doesn't it?

I also spend a lot of time talking to students and visiting schools. And the lack of study skills training is woefully obvious, whether the school is in the poorest section of town or the richest, in the inner city or suburban heaven, public or private, elementary, junior high or high school.

Teachers talk, kids are supposed to take notes on what they say. But I've never seen a teacher bother to teach the kids *how* to take good notes.

They test—oh, how they test! It's gotten to the point where teachers are spending more time teaching kids what's going to be on a standardized test than the particulars they should be learning. But many still don't teach any kind of test-taking strategies. When do you guess? What do you answer first, the easiest questions or the hardest? How do you get points on an essay question if you only have time to write a couple of sentences?

19

How to Study

You name the study skill, I can recite a few dozen horror stories. And, yes, I *am* trying to scare you. I'm trying to scare you into believing that your involvement in your child's education is absolutely essential to his or her eventual success. Surprisingly enough, the results of every study done in the last two decades about what affects a child's success in school concludes that only one factor *overwhelmingly* affects it, every time: parental involvement. Not the size of the school, the number of language labs, how many of the student body go on to college, how many great teachers there are (or lousy ones). All factors. *But none as significant as the effect **you** can have.*

So please, take the time to read ***How to Study*** yourself. Learn what your kids *should* be learning. Go over the results of the self-test in the next chapter—it will illuminate in glaring neon the areas your child *doesn't know*, which should certainly help you figure out what value you can be. (And which of the other six books in the series your child needs the most.) And if you discover you, your child and I are the only ones interested in learning how to study, take the teachers and school to task! The more parents rage about the abominable job our schools are doing, the more likely things will change.

And you can help tremendously, *even if you were not a great student yourself, even if you never learned great study skills*. You can learn now together with your child—not only will it help him or her in school, it will help *you* on the job, whatever your job.

Even if you think you need help only in a single area—or two or three—don't use only the specific book in my program that highlights that subject. Read ***How to Study*** first, *all the way through*. First of all, it will help you increase your mastery of skills you thought you already had. And it will cover those you need help with in a more concise manner. With that background, you will get *more* out of whichever of the other six books you use.

Presuming you need all the help all seven books can give you, what order should you read them in? Aside from reading ***How to Study*** first, I don't think it matters. All of the study skills are interrelated, so practicing one already helps you with the others. If pushed, however, I will admit that I would suggest **Improve Your Reading** and **Manage Your Time** be the first two books you study. The former because reading is the basis of every study skill, the latter because organization is the foundation on which the study pyramid is erected. After that, take your pick!

If you're a nontraditional student

If you're going back to high school, college or graduate school at age 25, 45, 65 or 85—you probably need the help in **How to Study** more than anyone! The longer you've been out of school, the more likely you don't remember what you've forgotten. And you've forgotten what you're supposed to remember! As much as I emphasize that it's rarely too early to learn good study habits, I must also emphasize that it's never too *late*.

What you *won't* find in How to Study

I've seen so-called study books spend chapters on proper nutrition, how to dress, how to exercise, and a number of other topics that are *not* covered *at all* in **How to Study,** except for this briefest of all acknowledgments: It is an absolute given that diet, sleep, exercise, use of drugs (including nicotine and caffeine) and alcohol all affect studying, perhaps significantly.

Having said that, I see little reason to waste your time detailing what should be obvious: Anything—including studying—is more difficult if you're tired, hungry, unhealthy, drunk, stoned, etc. So please use common sense. Eat as healthy as you can, get whatever sleep your body requires, stay reasonably fit and avoid alcohol and drugs. If your lack of success is in any way due to one of these other factors and you're unable to deal with it alone, find a good book or a professional to help you.

I think we've spent enough time talking about what you're *going* to learn. Let's get on with the learning.

Chapter One

HOW TO START OUT RIGHT

It is not enough to understand what we ought
to be, unless we understand what we are; and
we do not understand what we are, unless we
know what we ought to be.
— T. S. Eliot

Taking a good, honest look at yourself is not the easiest thing
in the world to do. In the next two chapters, I'm going to help you
evaluate the current level of all your study skills, a necessary step
to identify the areas in which you need to concentrate your efforts;
identify the study environment and learning style that suit you;
and categorize all of your school subjects according to how well
you *like* them and how well you *do* in them.

In the next few pages, I'm going to explain the 10 primary
study skill areas covered in this book: reading and comprehension, memory development, time management, library

skills, textbook note-taking, classroom note-taking, taking notes in the library, classroom participation, writing papers and test preparation. Then I'm going to ask you to rate yourself on your current level of achievement and understanding of these important skills: "A" for mastery or near mastery of a particular skill; "B" for some mastery; "C" for little or none.

Remember: There are no right or wrong answers in this assessment—no pass/fail determination. It's only a place to start, a jumping-off point from which you can measure your progress and rate those areas in which your skills need improvement.

I've listed the primary study skills below. Take a separate piece of paper and rate yourself on each of the 10 skills (from reading to test preparation) *before you read the rest of this chapter.* After you've rated yourself in each area, give yourself two points for every A, one point for every B, zero points for every C. If your overall rating is 15 or more, excellent (give yourself an A); 10 to 14, good (give yourself a B); and if nine or less, fair (give yourself a C). Mark this rating under Initial Study Skills Evaluation.

Now, let's review each of these areas, giving you insight as to what "fair," "good" and "excellent" really mean. As you read each section, go ahead and fill in your rating on the chart on page 19—and be honest with yourself. This evaluation will give you a benchmark from which to measure your improvement after you have completed the book. File it away and make the comparison when you've completed reading.

Your starting point

Initial Study Skills Evaluation   A ( )   B ( )   C ( )

Reading   A ( )   B ( )   C ( )

Memory Development   A ( )   B ( )   C ( )

Time Management   A ( )   B ( )   C ( )

Textbook Note-Taking   A ( )   B ( )   C ( )

How to Study

Classroom Note-Taking	**A ( )**	**B ( )**	**C ( )**
Classroom Participation	**A ( )**	**B ( )**	**C ( )**
Basic Library Skills	**A ( )**	**B ( )**	**C ( )**
Library Note-Taking	**A ( )**	**B ( )**	**C ( )**
Writing Papers	**A ( )**	**B ( )**	**C ( )**
Test Preparation	**A ( )**	**B ( )**	**C ( )**
Overall Study Skill Level	**A ( )**	**B ( )**	**C ( )**

Reading

Speed, comprehension and recall are the three important components of reading. Comprehension and recall are especially interrelated—better to sacrifice some speed to increase these two factors. To test your reading and comprehension skills, read the passage below, close the book and jot down the one, two or more key points made in the selection you read, then review the text and compare your notes with the reading selection. You will get a good idea of how well you understood what you read and just how good your top-of-the-mind recall is.

Like scientists, interviewers are now expected to gather similar types of information on all the specimens they study—information that can be measured, quantified and more easily and accurately compared. In fact, sometimes it seems as if quantification has replaced *qualification* in the hiring process.

The reasons are not as much Orwellian as economic. The "cost of hire"—the amount of money it takes to land a suitable candidate for a job—has escalated dramatically and will continue to increase as a result of the baby bust and the much ballyhooed shrinkage of the work force.

In addition, lawsuits against employers for wrongful discharge and other employment-related causes have increased exponentially over the past decade, making it more important for companies to hire people they (hope they) won't want to get rid of.

And, last but not least, for companies in our new Service Economy, the human resource is unquestionably the most valuable in their inventories.

For all of these reasons, interviewing is going to get tougher and tougher for job candidates at *all* levels of experience. You probably will have to go through more interviews than your predecessors—whatever job you are after, whatever your level of expertise—as well as tests designed to measure your honesty, intelligence, mental health and blood toxicity. (Employers seem to feel there's nothing worse than entry-level people on drugs, whatever your profession.)

Score: If you can read the material straight through and accurately summarize what you've read, all in less than two minutes, give yourself an A. If you have some problems reading and understanding the text but are able to complete the assignment in less than five minutes, give yourself a B. If you are unable to complete the assignment in that time, remember what you read or produce accurate notes at all, give yourself a C.

Retention

There are specific methods to help you recall when you must remember a lot of specific facts. One of these is memorization—committing information to word-for-word recall. Memorize only when you are required to remember something for a relatively short time.

When memorization is required, you should do whatever is necessary to impress the exact information on your mind. Repetition is probably the most effective method. The key, it has been determined, is to repeat the memory sequence of study, then recall. Language students, for example, have been taught to string together sentences in what soon becomes a short story or dialogue. Each day, new words are added and the student is required to remember and "parrot" them back the succeeding day. This add-on process has the effect of both stretching the memory (to make its capacity larger) and exercising it (to make the recall mechanism work more effectively).

Test #1: Look at the number following this paragraph for ten seconds. Then cover the page and write down as much of it as you can remember:

762049582049736

Test #2: Below are 12 "nonsense" words from a language I just made up and their "definitions." Study the list for 60 seconds in an attempt to remember each word, how it's spelled and its definition:

Bruhe	Thigh	**Trouch**	Chew
Imbor	Read	**Laved**	Man
Timp	Book	**Yout**	Head
Batoe	Runner	**Frewie**	Elbow
Plitter	Think	**Slecum**	Jacket
Kruk	Kitchen	**Preb**	Twist

Done? Close the book and write down each of the 12 words and its definition. They do not need to be in the order in which they were listed.

Score: Test # 1: If you remembered 12 or more digits in the correct order, give yourself an A; 8 to 12, a B; 7 or less, a C.

Test # 2: If you accurately listed eight or more words and definitions (and that includes spelling my new words correctly), give yourself an A. If you listed from five to seven words and their definitions or correctly listed and spelled more than eight words but mixed up their definitions, give yourself a B. If you were unable to remember at least four words and their definitions, give yourself a C.

Time management

Your effective use of available study time can be measured by two yardsticks: 1) your ability to break down assignments into component parts (e.g., reading, note-taking, outlining, writing); and, 2) your ability to complete each task in an efficient manner. The following questions will help you assess how well you are allocating your time, how organized you really are:

A. How many assignments have you failed to complete in the last month because you forgot when they were due, lacked required materials when you needed them or got to the library too late to read the assigned books?

B. Do you have a weekly or monthly calendar?

C. Do you always carry it with you?

D. How much time do you devote to study per week?

E. How many "all-nighters" (or *near*-all-nighters) did you pull in the last month?

Score: A. Give yourself one point for every such assignment; subtract five points if your answer is none.

B. *Add* five points for a "no" answer; *subtract* five points for a "yes."

C. *Add* two points for a "no"; *subtract* two for a "yes."

D. *Add* five points if you don't know; two points for less than four hours if in high school, less than 10 hours if in college; zero points for less than 10 hours in high school, less than 20 hours in college. *Subtract* one point for scheduled time greater than 10 hours in high school, 20 hours in college; five points if you study that hard but are convinced anyone else

How to Study

would have to study twice as long to accomplish what you do in half the time.

E. *Add* one point for each all-nighter or near-all-nighter. *Subtract* one point if "none." *Subtract* five points if your answer is "none" *and* you're an A or B student.

Use the chart below to see how you rate and how to grade yourself on this particular skill:

Test Score	Rating	Skill Score
-22 to -5	Excellent	A
- 4 to 0	Very good	A
1 - 5	Good	B
6 - 10	Fair	B
11 and up	Poor	C

Library skills

Using the library is a function of understanding its organization—and *using* it!. The more time you spend in the library—studying, reading, researching—the more productive you will be. You'll become adept at tracking down reference materials and finding the information you need quickly.

Virtually all libraries follow the same organization—once you understand it, you'll be "library literate," no matter which library you use. In this book, you'll discover what kinds of resources are available (books, periodicals, directories, encyclopedias, dictionaries, magazines, newspapers, documents, microfilm files), you'll learn how to select and find books (learning the Dewey Decimal and Library of Congress Systems) and you'll find out about the functions of the library staff.

To better evaluate your library skills, answer the following questions:

A. What collections are restricted in your library?

B. Where would you find a biography of Herbert Hoover in your local library?

C. Where is the reference section in your local library?

D. Given the Dewey number for a book, could you find it in less than five minutes? The LC number?

E. How often have you been to the library in the past six months? The past month?

Score: If the answers to these questions are all obvious to you, indicating a steady pattern of library use, then you can claim to have the library habit—give yourself an A. If you can't answer one or more of the questions or will freely own up to a spotty record of library use, give yourself a B. If you don't have the faintest clue of where the closest library is, you get a C.

Note-taking

Three different arenas—at home with your textbooks, the classroom, the library—require different methods of note-taking.

From your textbooks: Working from your books at home, you should identify the main ideas, rephrasing information in your own words, as well as capturing the details you were unfamiliar with. Take brief, concise notes in a separate notebook as you read. You should write down questions and answers to ensure your mastery of the material, starring those questions to which you *don't* have answers so you can ask them in class.

In class: Class *preparation* is the key to class *participation*. By reading material to be covered before you come to class, you will be able to concentrate and absorb the teacher's interpretations and points. Using a topical, short sentence approach or your own shorthand or symbols, take notes on those items that will trigger thematic comprehension of the subject matter. Your notes should be sequential, following the teacher's lecture pattern. When class is completed, review your notes at the first opportunity. Fill in the blanks and your own thoughts.

How to Study

In the library: What's the difference between taking notes at the library or working at home with library books vs. your own textbooks? Sooner or later you'll have to return library books (if you're allowed to take them out at all), and librarians tend to frown on highlighting them. So you need an effective system for library note-taking. In Chapter 7, I'll show you mine.

Score: If you feel that your note taking skills are sufficient to summarize necessary data from your textbooks, capture the key points from classroom lectures and discussions and allow you to prepare detailed outlines and write good papers, give yourself an A. If you feel any one of these three areas is deficient, give yourself a B. If notes are what you pass to your friends in class, give yourself a C.

Participating in class

I don't know too many teachers who don't take each student's class participation into account when giving grades, no matter how many spot quizzes they pull or how many term papers they assign. And, you may have discovered, there are teachers out there who will mark down students who "ace" every paper and quiz if they seem to disappear in the classroom.

Score: If you are always prepared for class—which means, at the very least, reading all assigned material, preparing assigned homework and projects and turning them in when due—actively participate in discussions and ask frequent and pertinent questions as a way of both trumpeting what you already know and filling in the gaps in that knowledge, give yourself an A. If you fail in any of these criteria, give yourself a B. If you aren't sure where the classroom is, give yourself a C.

Writing papers

Preparing any sort of report, written or oral, is 90 percent perspiration (research) and 10 percent inspiration (writing). In other words, the ability to write a good paper is more dependent on your mastery of the other skills we've already discussed than your mastery of *writing*. If you are an avid reader, familiar with your local library, a good note-taker and capable of breaking down the most complex topic into the manageable steps necessary to write a paper, you probably turn in superior papers.

Score: If you have already given yourself an "A" in Library Skills, Library Note Taking, Time Management and Reading, give yourself an A. If you feel you turn in relatively good papers but definitely lack in any of these areas, give yourself a B. If your idea of writing a paper is photocopying the pertinent "Cliff Notes" and recopying the summary in your own handwriting, give yourself a C.

Test preparation

The key to proper test preparation is an accurate assessment of what material will be covered and what form the test will take. Weekly class quizzes usually cover the most recent material. Midterm and final examinations cover a much broader area—usually all the subject matter to date. Multiple-choice tests, essays, lists of math problems, science lab tests all require different preparation and applying different test-taking skills. Knowing the kind of test you're facing will make your preparation much easier.

So will creating your own list of questions you think your teacher will most likely ask. Through periodic review of your text and class notes, the areas in which your teacher appears most interested—and on which he or she is most likely to test you—should begin to stand out. As a final trick, prepare a list of 10 or more questions *you* would ask if the roles were reversed and *you* were the teacher.

Score: If you are able to construct tests that are harder than the ones your teacher gives you—and you perform well on those—give yourself an A.

How to Study

If you feel you know the material, but somehow don't perform as well as you think you should come test time, give yourself a B.

If you didn't pass your driver's test, let alone algebra, give yourself a C.

Your overall score

Once again, after you've rated yourself in each area, give yourself two points for every A, one point for every B, zero points for every C. If your overall rating is 15 or more, excellent (give yourself an A); 10 to 14, good (give yourself a B); and if 9 or less, fair (give yourself a C). Put your new score in the section "Overall Study Skills Level" in the chart on page 24.

Now what?

The fact that you have been honest with yourself in evaluating those talents you bring into the study game is a big plus in your favor. Knowing where you are strong and where you need to improve makes everything else a good deal easier. Now, based on your test results, draw up a list of your assets and liabilities—your areas of strength and weakness. This will focus your attention on those areas that will require the most work to improve. As an example, a typical assessment might look something like this:

Study skills balance sheet

Good	Fair
Time management	Memory development
Library skills	Class participation
Note taking	Reading
Test preparation	Writing papers

Interpreting your results

Assuming for the moment that this is *your* study skills balance sheet, what can we learn from it? Apparently you are relatively organized, familiar with and comfortable using the library, and get a good deal out of classroom lectures, your reading and library research. And you test well—or, at least, prepare well. So some key skills are already in place.

On the other hand, you don't read as much as you should and have trouble comprehending and remembering what you do. Your classroom note-taking ability seems to have been developed at the cost of full participation. And your ability to take notes and use the library has yet to result into good papers.

Congratulations! While I would strongly recommend you read the entire book, this simple test has enabled you to identify the chapters you really need to work on—in this case, Chapters 3, 5 and 7—and the specific skills that may require work long after you finish reading this book.

Once you identify which study skills you need to develop, you can then take your efforts one step further. After you finish reading *How to Study*, continue to read any of the other six books in my **HOW TO STUDY** *Program* that apply to your needs: *"Ace" Any Test, Improve Your Memory, Improve Your Reading, Manage Your Time, Take Notes* and *Write Papers.*

Chapter Two

HOW TO ORGANIZE YOUR STUDYING

What effect can good study habits have? Certainly native-born talents and skills—the basic abilities you're born with—have the most to do with success in school. Fifty percent. Maybe 60. And the environment in which you're trying to learn, your health and other such factors may be another 10 percent, maybe 15. That leaves 25 to 40 percent for study skills.

Don't believe that learning how to study can have such a monstrous effect? Two comments: One, try me. Read **How to Study**, practice the skills, watch the results. I think you'll discover I'm right. Second, if you don't believe study skills are so important, you must be giving more weight to ability, kind of a "smart kids do well because they're smart" approach. Well, a lot of smart kids *don't* do well. At *all*. Others do well in school but test poorly. And many are great in some subjects and not-so-great in others. I don't have to prove this. Look at your friends, at others in your school. I guarantee you'll prove it yourself.

What kind of effort are we talking about here? Another hour a night? Two hours a night? *More???* And what about that "Study Smarter, Not Harder" slogan that's plastered all over the bookstore display for the **HOW TO STUDY** *Program*. "If I'm studying longer," you might reasonably contend, "I'm sure as heck studying harder, at least by my definition."

Let's take the latter point first. You *can* study smarter. You *can* put in less time and get better results. But learning how to do so *is* hard, because learning of *any* kind takes discipline. And learning self-discipline is, to many of us, the most difficult task of all. So don't kid yourself: You aren't going to sit down, read *How to Study*, and miraculously transform yourself from a "C" student to an "A" student. But you absolutely can if you put in the time to learn the lessons *Study* contains and, more importantly, to practice and use them every day.

And if you're currently doing little or nothing in the way of school work, then you *are* going to have to put in more time and effort. How much more? As much as you must to get the results you want to achieve. The smarter you are and the more easily you learn and adapt the techniques in *Study*, the more likely you will be spending less time on your homework than before. But the further you need to go—from Ds to As rather than Bs to As—the more you need to learn and the longer you need to give yourself to learn it.

Make study habit-forming

If you're doing poorly in school and you're actually putting in a reasonable amount of study time, you've got poor study habits. Lord knows where or when you acquired them, but failure has, to some extent, become a habit.

This is good news! Because not only can *bad* habits be broken, but they can be replaced by *good* habits relatively easily. Here's your battle plan:

How to Study

- It's easier to *replace* a habit than to "break" it entirely. So don't attempt to "stop" poor study habits, just learn the good ones that replace them.
- Practice, practice, practice. There's no way around it, practice is the motor oil that lubricates any habit's engine. The more you do something, the more ingrained it becomes. Just ask any smoker—if you can still find one—how many times they lit a cigarette today without even noticing that they had done so!
- Tell friends and family of your decision to do better in school by honing your study skills. This is a trick that works for *some* people, who find that the added pressure is a good motivator. Smokers are notorious for doing this, hoping that the fear of embarrassment (of disappointing all those friends and family if they light up again) will be one more motivation to quit. For some of you, however, such a strategy simply adds *too much* pressure and is more likely to encourage *failure*. Use such a strategy if you know it will help, avoid it if you know it will hurt.
- You don't have to grind it out from Ds to As with no feedback. Obviously, there's a lot of distance you're traveling and you'll be seeing the effects of better study habits all along the way. And each effect you see just strengthens your resolve and makes it even easier to keep on going. To make sure you get a "motivational jolt" from every accomplishment, resolve to chart every inch of your progress, even if, like Robert Frost, you have miles to go before you sleep. Set up a chart on your wall on which you list "Today's Successes" *every day*. Remember the small steps you're taking—saving five minutes on a reading assignment, finding the books you needed at the library more quickly, feeling you took good notes in a class, raising your hand to answer a question in class, etc.

Some overall study strategies

Starting with the next chapter, everything will concentrate on specific strategies useful in specific tasks—reading, note-taking, test-taking, etc. So this is probably the only place to discuss some overall strategies that have little to do with any particular task and everything to do with achieving overall study success:

Get ready to become a "lifer"

Learning how to study is really a long-term process. Once you undertake the journey, you will be surprised at the number of landmarks, pathways, side streets and road signs you'll find. Even after you've transformed yourself into a better student than you'd ever hoped to be, you'll inevitably find one more signpost that offers new information, one more pathway that leads you in an interesting new direction. Consider learning how to study a *lifelong process* and be ready to modify anything you're doing as you learn another method.

This is especially important right from the start when you consider your overall study strategies. How long you study per night, how long you work on a particular subject, how often you schedule breaks is going to vary considerably depending on how well you were doing before you read this book, how far you have to go, how interested you are in getting there, how involved you are in other activities, the time of day, your general health...Are you getting the idea?

It gets more complicated: What's your study sequence? Hardest assignments first? Easiest? Longest? Shortest? Are you comfortable switching back and forth from one to another or do you need to focus on a single assignment from start to finish?

This gets even more difficult (believe it or not!) when you consider that the tasks themselves may have a great affect on your schedule. When I sit down to plan out the chapter of a book, for example, I need a relatively long period of uninterrupted time—at least an hour, perhaps as long as three hours—in order to get my notes in the order I want them and to think through the entire chapter, writing transitions in my head, noting problem areas, figuring out where I need an example or illustration. If I only have half an hour before a meeting or appointment, I wouldn't even attempt to start such a project.

You may find yourself to be the same way and, therefore, need to ensure your schedule is flexible enough to adapt to the demands of the specific task. Fifteen-minute study unit increments might work well for you most of the time (though I suspect half an hour is an ideal unit for most of you, an hour only for those of you who can work that long without a break and who have assignments that traditionally take that long to complete). On the other hand, you may have no problem at all working on a long project in fits and starts, 15 or 20 minutes at a time, without needing to retrace your steps each time you pick it up again.

What's the lesson in all of this? There is no ideal answer, certainly no "right" answer, to many of the questions I've posed. It's a message you'll read in these pages over and over again: Figure out what works for you and keep on doing it. If it later stops working or doesn't work as well, change it. None of the study techniques discussed at such length in this book is carved in stone. You not only should feel free to adapt and shape and bend them to your own needs, you *must* do so.

Follow the Yellow Brick Road

When I talk about test-taking, one of the key bits of advice is to read the instructions before you start the test. This helps you avoid the poor grade (not to mention the frustration and embarrassment) that results from trying to answer all six essay questions in an hour when you were only supposed to pick three.

Tests aren't the only time "reading the instructions" is important. Many teachers have their own rules and regulations about turning in homework assignments, preparing papers (name in upper right-hand corner, double-spaced, one-inch margins all around, etc.) or projects, reporting lab results, etc. And it's just as important to follow these instructions—and just as devastating if you *don't*.

I really did have a teacher in 10th grade—when none of us had access to personal computers and few of us had yet learned to type—who failed a student because her paper was handwritten. What bothered me then was that the paper was really *good*...and it didn't mean a hill of beans to that teacher. Leaving aside for now the argument that the teacher was a bit too hung up on style to the detriment of substance (since I could equally argue that she was teaching important lessons about presentation and assumptions), isn't it ridiculous to get a low grade for such a lousy reason?

Be proud of your work...and show it

Do you know any students who make sure they count every word on their 500-word assignment and head to a conclusion as fast as they can as soon as they reach that magic number?

How about the student who is convinced his chicken scratch is perfectly decipherable, even when the teacher has to wade through several cross-outs on every page and follow arrows from one page to another because the student thought the order should be changed after the fact?

Or those who only spell one thing correctly per paper—their name—or, even worse, spell a word correctly two or three times and incorrectly four or five others, all on the same page?

Teachers are human. They respond to presentation. While I am not advocating an emphasis on form over substance, one should certainly consider that if the substance of two papers or tests or projects is relatively equal, the form in which they're presented may well affect the grade, perhaps significantly.

How to Study

Besides, there are a lot of teachers who make it a point to decrease grades because of poor grammar, spelling, presentation, etc. (And others who may subconsciously increase grades—or give a better grade than the work really warrants—because the presentation was done with care and a sense of pride.)

Practicing your Columbo impression

Teachers are different, too, in their approach to their subjects, their expectations, standards, flexibility, etc. It certainly is worth the effort to compile a "profile" of each of your teachers: What do each of them want to see in terms of notes, level of participation, papers, projects? What are their individual likes and dislikes? Their methods of grading and testing?

Knowing these various traits should certainly lead you to some adaptation of your approach to each class. Let's say—not that it would ever *really* happen to *you*, of course—that you have managed to dig yourself a very deep hole. It's 11 p.m., you're well past your study prime, and you still have reading assignments to complete for English and history tomorrow morning.

Your English teacher demands maximum class participation and makes it a large part of your grade—and your test scores be damned. Her hobby seems to be calling on the unprepared, and she seems to have an uncanny and unerring knack for ferreting them out.

Your history teacher discourages discussion, preferring to lecture and answer a couple of questions at the end of the class. He never calls on anyone for anything. Given this situation, and knowing you can stay awake long enough to read only one of the two assignments, which would it be?

In fact, presuming you care at all about your studies and grades, would there *ever* be a time, barring a simultaneous typhoon, eclipse and national holiday, that you would show up for that English class unprepared?

While I'll show you in Chapter 4 how to ensure that poor scheduling does not become a habit that leads to such choices, I suspect far too many of you do not take the natural differences among your various teachers into account when scheduling homework, preparing papers or studying for tests.

Likewise, I suspect far too few of you attempt to create a bond with one special teacher—a mentoring relationship—that could well help you avoid some of the bumps and swerves and make it to your goal with far less trouble. Why should you go out of your way to find a mentor? Because you probably need more help—in life, not just in school—than your friends or parents can provide. A mentor can give you that perspective, advice and help.

Intrinsic and extrinsic motivation

Motivators are either intrinsic or extrinsic. What's the difference? You sign up for a voice class. While the hours certainly apply to your graduating requirements, you attend class because you love singing.

You also signed up for biology. You hate the thought of dissecting frogs, and you couldn't care less whether they have exoskeletons, endoskeletons, hydroskeletons or no skeletons at all, but the class is required.

In the first scenario, you are motivated by *intrinsic* factors—you are taking the voice class because you enjoy it.

The second scenario is an example of *extrinsic* motivation. While you have no interest in biology, your reward for taking the class is external—you will be able to graduate.

Extrinsic motivation can help you make it through the boring or unpleasant tasks that are necessary to reach your goals. A vivid, visual image of your final goal can be a powerful motivating force. For example, one student thought about what his job as a computer programmer would be like whenever he needed a little help getting through class.

41

How to Study

Try imagining what a day in *your* life will be like five or 10 years down the road. If you haven't the faintest clue, no *wonder* you're having a hard time motivating yourself to work toward that career as a final goal!

The goal pyramid

One way to easily visualize all your goals—and their relation to each other—is to construct what I call a *goal pyramid*. Here's how to do it:

1. Centered at the top of a piece of paper, write down what you hope to ultimately gain from your education. This is your long-range goal and the pinnacle of your pyramid. Example: Become a successful advertising copywriter.

2. Below your long-range goal(s), list mid-range goals—milestones or steps that will lead you to your eventual target. For example, if your long-range goal were to become an advertising copywriter, your mid-range goals might include getting into college, "acing" all your writing courses, completing all required courses and getting a summer internship at a major ad agency.

3. Below the mid-range goals, list as many short-range goals as you can—smaller steps that can be completed in a relatively short period of time. For example, if your long-range goal is to become a travel writer, your mid-range goal may be to earn a degree in journalism. Short-range goals may include writing a travel article for the school paper, registering for magazine writing courses or doing well in a related class.

Change your goal pyramid as you progress through school. You may eventually decide on a different career. Or your mid-range goals may change as you decide on a different path leading to the long-range goal. The short-range goals will undoubtedly change, even daily.

The process of creating your own goal pyramid allows you to see *how* all those little daily and weekly steps you take can lead to your mid-range and long-term goals, and will thereby motivate you to work on your daily and weekly tasks with more energy and enthusiasm.

Make goal-setting a part of your life

The development of good study skills is the highway to your goals, whatever they are. And no matter how hard you have to work or how much adversity you have to overcome along the way, the journey will indeed be worth it.

How do you make setting goals a part of your life? Here are some hints I think will help:

1. ***Be realistic*** when you set goals. Don't aim too high or low and don't be particularly concerned when (not if) you have to make adjustments along the way.

2. ***Be realistic about your expectations***. An improved understanding of a subject you have little aptitude for is preferable to getting hopelessly bogged down if total mastery of the subject is just not in the cards.

3. ***Beware the Goldilocks Conundrum***. Despite the previous two points, you can be *overly* realistic—too ready to sigh and give up just because something is just "too hot" or "too cold". There's a fine line between aiming too high and feeling miserable when you don't come close, aiming too low and never achieving your potential, and finding the path that's right for you.

4. ***Concentrate on areas that offer the best chance for improvement***. Unexpected successes

can do wonders for your confidence and might make it possible for you to achieve more than you thought in other areas.

5. ***Monitor your achievements and keep resetting your goals.*** Daily, weekly, monthly, yearly—ask yourself how you've done, where you'd like to go *now*.

Use rewards as artificial motivators

The way you decide to use a reward system all depends on how much help you need getting motivated to study. As we've observed, tasks that are intrinsically interesting require little outside motivation. However, most schoolwork can be spurred along by the promise of little rewards along the way. If the task is especially tedious or difficult, make the rewards more frequent so that motivation doesn't sag.

As a general rule, the size of the reward should match the difficulty of the task. For an hour of reading, promise yourself a 10-minute walk. For completion of a rough draft for a big assignment, treat yourself to a movie.

Carrot or stick?

In trying to motivate yourself, do you tend to use the carrot or the stick? Positive and negative thoughts can both motivate.

The following are examples of *negative* thoughts that students have used to motivate themselves:

1. "If I don't get a good mark on this test, there goes my grade."
2. "If I don't finish this assignment, I'll have to miss the party."
3. "If I blow this college entrance exam, my future is shot."
4. "I'll be forced to go to summer school if I don't do well in this class."

Now here are some examples of *positive* thoughts that students have used to motivate themselves:

1. "For every hour of solid study, I get to listen to two songs on my new CD."
2. "If I get this assignment done early, I will be able to go skiing Friday."
3. "If I earn an A in this class, I'll reward myself with a weekend at the beach."
4. "If I do well in these courses, my chances for grad school are excellent."

There is no rule against using the stick to motivate yourself. But, you should learn to turn your failures into successes. This will keep your attitude positive and keep the wind in your sails. Focusing on the positive helps you feel good about yourself and provides excitement to keep you motivated.

How perfect are you?

What is a perfectionist, and are you one? And if you are, why is it a problem? (If you answered "no" to the first two questions, you can freely skip this section. I suspect I'm speaking to a minority of my readers here.)

Remember our earlier discussion about "showing you care" and taking the time to "do things right"? Perfectionists care perhaps *too* much, finding it impossible to be satisfied with anything less than "perfect" work (as they define it), presuming for a moment that such an ideal can actually be attained.

It is possible, of course, to score a "perfect" 100 on a test or to get an A+ on a paper the teacher calls "Perfect!" in the margin. But in reality, doing anything "perfectly" is an impossible task.

What does all this have to do with you? Nothing, unless you find yourself spending two hours polishing an already A+

paper or half an hour searching for that one "perfect" word or an hour rewriting great notes to make them "absolutely perfect." In other words, while striving for perfection may well be a notable trait, it can very easily, perhaps inevitably, become a major problem if it becomes an uncontrollable and unstoppable urge that seriously inhibits your enjoyment of your work and your life.

Take it from a perfectionist. It's easy (though still not necessarily great) to "be a perfectionist" when you're in the elementary grades. But just try to attend class and labs (as I did) 38 hours a week, work nearly full-time and, of course, do the 50-plus hours of homework per week, all while wasting *days* "searching for that perfect word!" There comes a time—hopefully, for your sake, sooner rather than later—when you must simply conclude that you cannot *afford* to be a perfectionist. That taking two hours to make a paper "perfect" when the three word changes you decided upon made absolutely no difference to your grade (or the caliber of your work or your understanding of the subject) is a *big waste of time.*

I'm convinced that there aren't too many of you out there nodding your head and thinking, "Oh, yeah, that's me!" But I'm equally convinced that those of you to whom this all makes sense are making your lives incredibly tough. If you are perfectionistic—a little or a lot—recognize that trait and take the necessary steps to rein it in when you want (or need) to. If you really would prefer spending another couple of hours "polishing" that A+ paper to taking in a movie, reading a book or getting some *other* assignment done, be my guest.

Creating *your* study environment

The time is 9:30 p.m. A Pearl Jam CD is cranked up. Your books and notes are strewn across the floor in no particular order. The history test is scheduled for 9 a.m. tomorrow and you haven't looked at the textbook in a week. You've promised your mother you'll take out the garbage and walk the dog. You were up late watching a favorite TV show last night and you're still tired.

With all these distractions, the noise level, other commitments and general fatigue, you're not exactly heading for quality study time. And that's the point: Within such an environment, time spent will most likely be time wasted. How will you concentrate with loud music? How will you focus on the retention, recognition and recall process when your eyelids are kissing? Will you be called away at a critical moment to walk the dog?

Now imagine the following scenario: You've found a quiet corner at a reading table in your local library. You just left class and plan to review your history notes while they're still fresh in your mind. You look around you. All heads are down—focusing, concentrating, thinking. This is a *study* environment—you are not separated from the activities of others, but rather a willing participant in a seemingly universal pattern. Now you're ready for *quality* study time.

In half the time you had scheduled, you finish your reading, sift the material, make your notes and head for home.

This comparison of good and bad study environments is so simple as to be self-evident, you'd think. Amazingly, the negative situation portrayed is all too often the case. If it's one *you're* more familiar with, it's time to change. You need the right skills and the right environment if you are to be successful. But the right environment for you is probably the wrong one for someone else. Do you know where, when and how *you* study best?

In the library? At home? At a friend's? Before dinner? After dinner? When it's quiet? Noisy? With music? With the TV on? Easiest assignments first? Hardest? Reading before writing?

Check it out

On page 49, I have included a checklist for you to rate your study environment. It includes not just *where* you study—at home, in the library, at a friend's—but *when* and *how* you study, too. Once you've identified what works for you, avoid those situations in which you now *know* you don't perform best. If you don't know the answer to one or more of the questions, take the time to experiment.

(For more information about creating the ideal study environment, be sure to read ***Manage Your Time.***)

Many of the items on this chart should be understandable to you now. Remember: *Why* you feel the need for a particular environment is not important. Knowing that you *have a preference* is. Here's what you're trying to assess in each item:

1. If you prefer "listening" to "seeing," you'll have little problem getting the information you need from class lectures and discussion. In fact, you'll *prefer* them to studying your textbooks. (You may have to concentrate on your reading skills and spend more time with your textbooks to offset this tendency. Highlighting your texts may help.)

If you're more of a "visual" person, you'll probably find it easier reading your textbook and may have to work to improve your classroom concentration. Taking excellent class notes that you can read later will probably be important for you. You'll also want to adapt your note-taking methods to your visual preference—rather than writing notes like everybody else, draw pictures, use charts and learn how to "map" a lecture. (See Chapters 5 and 7 for a complete discussion of note-taking techniques.)

2. This should tie in with your answer to (1). The more "aural" you are, the more you should concentrate on listening. The more "visual," the better your notes should be for later review.

3. This may make a difference for a number of reasons. You may find it difficult to hear or see from the back of the classroom. You may be shy and want to sit up front to make yourself participate. You may find sitting near a window makes you feel less claustrophobic; alternatively, you may daydream too much if near a window and should sit as far "inside" the classroom as possible.

My Ideal Study Environment

How I receive information best:

1. ❑ Orally ❑ Visually

In the classroom, I should:

2. ❑ Concentrate on taking notes ❑ Concentrate on
listening
3. ❑ Sit in front ❑ Sit in back ❑ Sit near window or door

Where I study best:

4. ❑ At home ❑ In the library ❑ Somewhere else:

_____

When I study best:

5. ❑ Every night; little on weekends ❑ Mainly on weekends
❑ Spread out over seven days
6. ❑ In the morning ❑ Evening ❑ Afternoon
7. ❑ Before dinner ❑ After dinner

How I study best:

8. ❑ Alone ❑ With a friend ❑ In a group
9. ❑ Under time pressure ❑ Before I know I have to
10. ❑ With music ❑ In front of TV ❑ In a quiet room
11. ❑ Organizing an entire night's studying before I start
❑ Tackling and completing one subject at a time

I need to take a break:

12. ❑ Every 30 minutes or so ❑ Every hour ❑ Every 2 hrs.
❑ Every ____ hours

How to Study

4. Whatever location you find most conducive to study—given the limitations of your living situation and schedule—should be where you spend the majority of your study time.

5. How to organize your time to most effectively cover the material: This may depend, in part, on the amount of homework you are burdened with and/or the time of year—you may have one schedule during most of the school year but have to adapt during test time, if papers are due, for special projects, etc.

6. To some of you, such preferences may only be a factor on weekends, because your day hours are set—you're in school.

But if you're in college (or in a high school program that mimics college's "choose your own courses and times" scheduling procedures), you would want to use this factor in determining when to schedule your classes.

If you study best in the morning, for example, try to schedule as many classes as possible in the afternoons (or, at worst, late in the morning).

If you study best in the evening, either schedule morning classes and leave your afternoons free for other activities, or schedule them in the afternoons so you can sleep later (and study later the night before).

7. Some of us get cranky if we try to do *anything* when we're hungry. If you study poorly when your stomach is growling, eat something!

8. Most of us grow up automatically studying alone. If we study with a friend, there's often more horseplay than studying. But don't underestimate the positive effect studying with one or two friends—or even a larger study group—can have on your mastery of schoolwork and on your grades. (I discuss study groups in greater detail at the end of this section.)

9. Just because you perform best under pressure doesn't mean you should always leave projects, papers and studying for tests until the last minute. It just means if you're well organized, but an unexpected project gets assigned or a surprise test announced, you won't panic.

If you do *not* study well under pressure, it certainly doesn't mean you occasionally won't be required to do so. The better organized you are, the easier it will be for you all the time, but especially when the unexpected arises.

10. As we've discussed, some of you (like me) will find it difficult to concentrate with*out* music or some sort of noise. Others couldn't sit in front of the TV and do *any*thing but breathe and eat. Many of you will fall in between—you can read and even take notes to music but need absolute quiet to study for a test or master particularly difficult concepts. If you don't know how you function best, now is the time to find out.

11. Back to organizing. The latter concept—starting and finishing one project before moving on to another—doesn't mean you can't at least sit down and outline an entire night's study plan before tackling each subject, one at a time. Setting up such a study schedule *is* advised. But it may mean you really *can't* move to another project while the one you're now working on is unfinished. Others of you may have no problem working on one project, switching to another when you get stuck or just need a break, then going back to the first.

12. There's nothing particularly wrong with taking a break whenever you feel you need to keep yourself sharp and maximize your quality study time...as long as the breaks aren't every five minutes and don't last longer than the study periods! In general, though, try to increase your concentration through practice so that you can go at least an hour before getting up, stretching and having a drink or snack. Too many projects will require at least that long to "get into" or organize, and you may find that breaking too frequently will require too much "review time" when you return to your desk.

Study groups: What are friends for?

Surprisingly enough, I was 35 and a devoted watcher of the television show "The Paper Chase" before I was introduced to the concept of a study group. Now this series was supposed to be about a law school that seemed just this side of hell, so sharing the load with other students wasn't just a good idea, it was virtually mandatory for survival. My high school certainly wasn't hell, not even a mild purgatory, but I think a study group would have been beneficial. If I had thought of the idea myself, even in high school, I would have started one.

The idea is simple: Find a small group of like-minded students—four to six seems to be an optimal number—and share notes, question each other, prepare for tests together. To be effective, obviously, the students you pick to be in your group should share all, or at least most, of your classes.

Search out students who are smarter than you, but not too much smarter. If they are on a level far beyond your own, you'll soon be left in the dust and be more discouraged than ever. On the other hand, if you choose students who are too far beneath your level, you may enjoy being the "brain"of the bunch but miss the point of the group—the challenge of other minds to spur you on.

Study groups can be organized in a variety of ways. Each member could be assigned primary responsibility for a single class, including preparing detailed notes from lectures and discussion groups. If supplementary reading is recommended but not required, that person could be responsible for doing all such reading and preparing detailed summaries.

Alternatively, everybody can be responsible for his or her own notes, but the group could act as an ad hoc discussion group, refining your understanding of key points, working on problems together, questioning each other, practicing for tests, etc.

Even if you find only one or two other students willing to work with you, such cooperation will be invaluable, especially in preparing for major exams.

Tips for forming your own study group

- I suggest four students minimum, probably six maximum. You want to ensure everyone gets a chance to participate as much as they want while maximizing the collective knowledge and wisdom of the group.

- While group members needn't be best friends, they shouldn't be overtly hostile to one another. Seek diversity of experience, demand common dedication.

- Try to select students that are at least as smart, committed and serious as you. That will encourage you to keep up and challenge you a bit. Avoid a group in which you're the "star"—at least until you flame out during the first exam.

- Avoid inviting members who are inherently unequal into the group—boyfriend/girlfriend combinations, in which one or the other may be inhibited by their *amore's* presence; situations where one student works for another; situations where underclassmen and upperclassmen may stifle one another; etc.

- Decide if you're forming a study group or a social group. If the latter, don't pretend it's the former. If the former, don't just invite your friends and sit around discussing your teachers for an hour a week.

- There are a number of ways to organize, as we briefly discussed above. My suggestion is to assign each class to one student. That student must truly master that assigned class, doing, in addition to the regular assignments, of course, any or all additional reading (recommended by the professor or not) necessary to achieve that goal, taking outstanding notes, outlining the course (if the group decides that would be helpful), being available for questions about specific topics in the class and preparing various practice quizzes, midterms and finals, as needed, to help test the other students' mastery.

Needless to say, all of the other students still attend all classes, take their own notes, do their own reading and homework assignments. But the student assigned that class attempts to learn as much as the professor, to actually be the "substitute professor" of that class in the study group. (So if you have five classes, a five-person study group becomes the ideal.)

- Make meeting times and assignments formal and rigorous. Consider rigid rules of conduct. For example, miss two meetings, whatever the excuse, and you're out. Better to shake out the nonserious students early. You don't want anyone who is working as little as possible but hoping to take advantage of *your* hard work.

- Consider appointing a chair (rotating, if you wish, weekly) in charge of keeping everyone to schedule and settling disputes before they disrupt the study group.

- However you organize, clearly decide—early—the exact requirements and assignments of each student. Again, you never want the feeling to emerge that someone is trying to "ride the coattails" of the others.

Where should *you* study?

At the library. And realize within the library there may be numerous choices, from the large reading room, to quieter, sometimes deserted specialty rooms, to your own study cubicle. My favorite "home away from home" at Princeton was a little room that seemingly only four or five of us knew about—with four wonderfully comfortable chairs, subdued lighting, phonographs with earplugs and a selection of some 500 classical records. For someone who needs music to study, it was custommade for me!

At home. Just remember that this is the place where distractions are most likely to occur. No one tends to telephone you at the library and little brothers (or your own kids) will not tend to find you easily in the "stacks." It is, of course, usually the most convenient place to make your study headquarters. It may not, however, be the most effective.

At a friend's, neighbor's or relative's. This may not be an option at all for most of you, even on an occasional basis, but you may want to set up one or two alternative study sites. Despite many experts' opinion that you must study in the same place every night (with which I don't agree), I have a friend who simply craves some variety to help motivate him. He has four different places he likes to study and simply rotates them from night to night. Whatever works for you.

In an empty classroom. Certainly an option at many colleges and perhaps some private high schools, it is an interesting idea mainly because so few students have ever thought of it! While not a likely option at a public high school, it never hurts to ask if you can't make some arrangements. Since many athletic teams practice until 6 p.m. or later, even on the high school level, there may well be a part of the school open—and usable with permission—even if the rest is locked up tight.

At your job. Whether you're a student working part-time or a full-timer going to school part-time, you may well be able to make arrangements to use an empty office, even during regular office hours, perhaps after everyone has left (depending on how much your boss trusts you). If you're in junior high or high school and a parent, friend or relative works nearby, you may be able to work from just after school until closing time at their workplace.

How to stay focused

Create a work environment in which* you're *comfortable. The size, style and placement of your desk, chair and lighting may all affect how easily (or poorly) you're distracted from the work at hand. Take the time to design the area that's perfect for you. Needless to say, anything that you know will distract you—a girlfriend's picture, a radio or TV, whatever, should disappear from your study area.

How to Study

Turn up the lights. Subtle, recessed lighting may be beautiful in a living room, but it is probably not highly effective for really concentrated study. Experiment with the placement and intensity of lighting in your study area until you find what works for you, both in terms of comfort and as a means of staying awake and focused.

Set some rules. Let family, relatives and especially friends know how important your studying is and that specific hours are inviolate. Many business executives rarely "take" phone calls— they simply let their assistants stack up the pink message slips and then, during a single hour, return the calls *they* want when it's most convenient for *them*. As one who generally does so, I can attest that it is a major time-saver. Most people invariably call when you're right in the middle of something; by the time you get off the phone, you have to go back and start over again. What a waste of precious study time!

Take the breaks you need. Don't follow some parent's or teacher's well-intentioned but bogus advice about how long you should study before taking a break. Take the breaks when *you* need to. If you're tired and just going through the motions, you're wasting your time, even if your last break was 15 minutes ago. Take another and psych yourself up for the next round!

Fighting tiredness and boredom

Take a nap. What a concept! When you're too tired to study, take a short nap to revive yourself. Seems pretty obvious, doesn't it? Nevertheless, you will undoubtedly find more misguided experts who feel "naps" are just for lazy people.

Hogwash. I am a confirmed afternoon napper, as is Henry Kissinger and as was Malcolm Forbes, neither of whom, I believe, were generally considered lazy.

The key is to maximize that nap's effect, and *that* means keeping it short—20 minutes is ideal, 40 minutes absolute maximum. After that, you go into another phase of sleep and you may well wake even more tired than before. If you can't take such short naps, train yourself to do so. I did during college out of absolute necessity. I consider my ability to nap virtually anywhere, anytime, and automatically wake after 20 minutes, one of my more useful talents.

Have a drink. A little caffeine won't harm you—a cup of coffee or tea, a glass of soda. Just be careful not to mainline it—caffeine's "wake-up" properties seem to reverse when you reach a certain level, making you far more tired than you were!

Turn down the heat. You needn't build an igloo out back, but too warm a room will inevitably leave you dreaming of sugarplums—while your paper remains unwritten on your desk.

Shake a leg. Or anything else that peps you up. Go for a walk, high step around the kitchen, do a few jumping jacks—even mild physical exertion will give you an immediate lift.

Change your study schedule. Presuming you have some choice here, find a way to study when *you* are normally more awake and/or most efficient.

Studying with small kids

So many more of you are going back to school while raising a family, I want to give you some ideas that will help you cope with the Charge of the Preschool Light Brigade:

Plan activities to keep the kids occupied. And out of your hair. The busier you are in school and/or at work, the more time your kids will want you when you *are* home. If you spend a little time with them, it may be easier for them to play alone, especially if you've planned ahead, creating projects *they* can work on while *you*'re working on your homework.

Make the kids part of your study routine. Kids love routine, so why not include them in yours? If 4 p.m. to 6 p.m. is always "Mommy's Study Time," they will soon get used to it, especially if you make spending other time with them a priority and if you take the time to give them something to do dur-

ing those hours. Explaining the importance of what you're doing—in a way that includes some ultimate benefit for *them*—
will also motivate them to be part of your "study team."

Use the television as a baby-sitter. While many of you
will have a problem with this—one that I and my 5-year-old
deal with weekly, if not daily—it may be the lesser of two evils.
And you can certainly rent (or tape) enough quality shows so
you don't have to worry about the little darlings are watching
Ninja Turtles bash skulls in (or bashing skulls themselves on
some video game system).

Plan your study accordingly. Unless you are right up
there in the Perfect Parent Pantheon, all of these things will
not keep your kids from interrupting every now and then.
While you can minimize such intrusions, it's virtually impossible to eliminate them entirely. So don't try—plan your
schedule *assuming* such interruptions. For one, that means
taking more frequent breaks to spend five minutes with your
kids. They'll be more likely to give you the 15 or 20 minutes at
a time *you* need if they get periodic attention themselves. By
default, *that* means avoiding projects that can only be done
with an hour of massive concentration—you can only work in
15 or 20 minute bursts!

Find help. Spouses can occasionally take the kids out for
dinner and a movie (and trust me, the kids will encourage you
to study *more* if you do this!), relatives can baby-sit (at their
homes) on a rotating basis, playmates can be invited over
(allowing you to send your darling to their house the next day),
you may be able to trade baby-sitting chores with other parents, and professional day-care may be available at your
child's school or in someone's home for a couple of hours a day.

Find out where *you* shine

It is the rare individual who is superior, or even good, in
every subject. If you are, count your blessings. Most of us are a
little better in one subject or another. Some of us simply *like*

one subject more than another—and don't think *that* doesn't change your attitude toward it. Others are naturally gifted in one area, average in others.

For example, skill with numbers and spatial relations may come easily to you. but you may have no ear for music or languages. Or you may find learning a language to be easy, but not have the faintest clue why Pythagoras came up with his Theorem—or why you should care. Some students are good with their hands. Others (again, like me) may find making the simplest item akin to torture.

The reasons for such unequal distribution of native-born talents rest somewhere in the area between karma and God, depending on your philosophy.

Presuming that most of us are good in one or two subjects, average or poor in others, we can react to this state of affairs in one of two ways: 1) Concentrate on those areas in which we're weakest and work to improve basic skills such as reading, memory and organization so as to minimize our lack of particular talents; or 2) concentrate exclusively on developing the particular skills we feel we like or need without worrying about the others at all.

Most of you would probably lean to the former solution. That's why you're plowing through this book, isn't it? And the skills you will learn, practice and strengthen throughout it will undoubtedly change your approach to subjects you currently dislike or just aren't good at. It will never enable you to add a string of numbers in your head faster than a calculator or start speaking a language with a native accent just by listening to the waiter in the local French restaurant. Unless those talents are in your genes. But it may give you the impetus to do better in math or learn French with a little less pain.

On the other hand, each of us has probably met someone who has taken the second course—strengthening his or her native-born talents and ignoring the rest. Such a person—salesman, computer guru, physician, etc.—may have reached an incredible plateau of success in his or her field. While being suitably impressed by their professional accomplishments, we may be astounded at their demonstrated ignorance of literature, current affairs, art, music or a number of other areas.

Should we criticize this person for concentrating solely on his or her strengths and doing it so successfully that he or she becomes a world-famous surgeon or the owner of a billion-dollar computer firm? Even if he or she never did do particularly well in English?

It's one way to get where you want to go. And may well be a path you choose.

My advice is to be thankful for whatever native-born talents you possess and use the gift as a two-edged sword. Shift some study time from those tasks easily achieved to those that you find more difficult. The balance you will see in your development will be well worth the effort.

And if you've never really thought about the subjects you like and dislike, use the chart on page 62 to identify them. You'll also be asked to identify those in which you perform well or poorly. (Your report card should confirm your list of those!) Use this list to organize your own schedule to take advantage of your natural talents and give added time to the subject areas that need the most work.

And if you have a choice

All college students—and some high school students—are able to pick and choose courses according to their own schedules, likes, dislikes, goals, etc. The headiness of such freedom should be tempered with the common-sense approach you're trying to develop through reading this book. Here are a few hints to help you along:

1. Whenever possible, consider each professor's reputation as you decide whether to select a particular course (especially if it is an overview or introductory

course that is offered in two or three sessions). Word gets around as to which professors' lectures are stimulating and rewarding—even if it isn't a subject you like!

2. Attempt to select classes so that your schedule is balanced on a weekly and even a daily basis, though this will not always be possible or advisable. (Don't change your major just to fit your schedule!) Try to leave an open hour or half-hour between classes— it's ideal for review, post-class note-taking, quick trips to the library, etc.

3. Try to alternate challenging classes with those that come more easily to you. Studying is a process of positive reinforcement. You'll need encouragement along the way.

4. Avoid late-evening or early-morning classes, especially if such scheduling provides you with large gaps of "down time."

5. Set a personal study pace and follow it. Place yourself on a study diet, the key rule of which is: *Don't overeat.*

The landscape is littered with the shadows of unsuccessful students who have failed in their pursuits—*not* because they lacked the talent or motivation, but because they just overloaded on information and pressure.

You *can* be successful without killing yourself!

Evaluation of Subject Areas

List the subject areas/courses you like most:

_____

_____

_____

_____

List those you like least:

_____

_____

_____

_____

List the courses in which you get the best grades:

_____

_____

_____

_____

And those in which you get the worst grades:

_____

_____

_____

_____

Chapter Three

HOW TO READ AND REMEMBER

Reading transforms and transports us through times past, present and future.

Nothing you will do as you pursue your studies will be as valuable as the reading skills you develop—they are your ultimate long-term learning tool.

Presuming you agree, what do you do?

This chapter will help you learn:

- The standard sections of books designed to help you and how to use them
- How to read material the right way (three types of reading)
- How fast (or slow) you should be reading
- How to take better notes in your textbooks and during your reading assignments

How to Study

- How to comprehend more of what you read
- How your memory works and what you can do to improve it
- How to build your own library of books and authors

I can only cover so much in one chapter. After reading this one, if you feel you need more help with your reading comprehension, I urge you to consult *Improve Your Reading* and *Improve Your Memory,* both of which have also just been released in new editions.

The shorthand of reading

There is a group of special sections found in nearly all textbooks and technical materials (in fact, in almost all books except novels) that contain a wealth of information and can help you glean more from your reading. Becoming familiar with this data will enrich your reading experience and often make it easier. Here's what to look for:

The first page after the title page is usually the *table of contents*—a chapter-by-chapter list of the book's contents. Some are surprisingly detailed, listing every major point or topic covered in each chapter.

The first prose section (after the title page, table of contents and, perhaps, acknowledgments page, in which the author thanks other authors and his or her editor, typist, researcher, friends, relatives, teachers, etc., most of which can be ignored by the reader), the *preface* is usually a description of what information you will find in the book. Authors may also use the preface to point out unique aspects of their books.

The *introduction* may be in place of or in addition to the preface and may be written by the author or some "name" the author has recruited to lend additional prestige to his or her work. Most introductions are an even more detailed overview of the book—chapter-by-chapter summaries are often included to give the reader a feel for the material to be covered.

Footnotes may be found throughout the text (a slightly elevated number following a sentence, quote etc., e.g., "jim dandy"[24]) and either explained at the bottom of the page on which they appear or in a special section at the back of the text. Footnotes may be used to cite sources of direct quotes or ideas and/or to further explain a point, add information, etc. outside of the text. You may make it a habit to ferret out sources cited in this way for further reading.

If a text tends to use an alarmingly high number of terms with which you may not be familiar, the considerate author will include a *glossary*—essentially an abridged dictionary that defines all such terms.

The *bibliography*, usually at the end of the book, may include the source material the author used to research the textbook, a list of "recommended reading" or both. It is usually organized alphabetically by subject, making it easy for you to go to your library and find more information on a specific topic.

Appendices containing supplementary data or examples relating to subject matter covered in the text may also appear in the back of the book.

The last thing in a book is usually the *index,* an alphabetical listing that references, by page number, every mention of a particular name, subject, topic, etc. in the text.

Making it a habit to utilize all of these tools in your textbooks can only make your studying easier.

Three ways to read

Depending on what you're trying to accomplish in a particular reading assignment and the kind of book involved, there are actually three different ways to read. Knowing when to use each will make any assignment easier:

1. ***Quick reference reading*** focuses on seeking specific information that addresses a particular question or concern we might have.

2. ***Critical reading*** is used to discern ideas and concepts that require a thorough analysis.

3. ***Aesthetic or pleasure reading*** is for sheer entertainment or to appreciate an author's style and ability.

Skim first, then read for detail

The best way to begin any reading assignment is to skim the pages to get an overall view of what information is included. Then read the text carefully, word-for-word, and highlight the text and/or take notes in your notebook. (A brief digression: Most everyone I know loves to confuse "skim" and "scan." Let me set the record straight. **Skim is to read quickly and superficially. Scan is to read carefully but for a specific item**. So when you skim a reading selection, you are reading it in its entirety, though you're only hitting the "highlights." When you scan a selection, you are reading it in detail but only until you find what you're looking for. Scanning is the *fastest* reading rate of all—although you are reading in detail, you are *not* seeking to comprehend or remember anything that you see until you find the bit of information you're looking for. I now trust none of you will ever confuse these words again!)

Newspapers make reading simple—most newspaper articles are written in the "pyramid" format. The first paragraph (at the top of the pyramid) makes the major point of the story. Succeeding paragraphs add more and more detail, filling out the pyramid. So gleaning the key news stories from a newspaper is as easy as reading the headlines and the first two or three paragraphs of each.

Your textbooks are not always written to facilitate such an approach, but most of the authors probably make their key point of any paragraph in the first sentence of that paragraph. Succeeding sentences add details. In addition, most of your textbooks include helpful "call outs"—those brief notes or headings in the outside margins of each page that summarize the topic covered in the paragraph or section. Or, like this book, include headings and subheadings to organize the material.

These standard organizational tools should make your reading job simpler. The next time you have to read a history, geography or similar text, try skimming the assigned pages first. Read the heads, the subheads and the call outs. Read the first sentence of each paragraph. Then go back and start reading the details.

To summarize the skimming process:

1. Read and be sure you understand the title or heading. Try rephrasing it as a question for further clarification of what you will read.
2. Examine all the subheadings, illustrations and graphics—these will help you identify the significant matter within the text.
3. Read *thoroughly* the introductory paragraphs, the summary at the end and questions at chapter's end.
4. Read the first sentence of every paragraph—this generally includes the main idea.
5. Evaluate what you have gained from this process: Can you answer the questions at the end of the chapter? Could you intelligently participate in a class discussion of the material?
6. Write a brief summary that capsulizes what you have learned from your skimming.
7. Based on this evaluation, decide whether a more thorough reading is required.

Now go back for detail

If a more thorough reading is then required, turn back to the beginning. ***Read one section (chapter, etc.) at a time.***

And do not go on to the next until you've completed the following exercise:

1. Write definitions of any key terms you feel are essential to understanding the topic.
2. Write questions and answers you feel clarify the topic.
3. Write any questions for which you *don't* have answers—then make sure you find them through rereading, further research or asking another student or your teacher.
4. Even if you still have unanswered questions, move on to the next section and complete numbers 1 to 3 for that section. (And so on, until your reading assignment is complete.)

See if this method doesn't help you get a better handle on any assignment right from the start.

The method you probably learned

If you were taught any specific reading method in school, it was probably the one developed back in the 1940s that is abbreviated "SQ3R." This stands for **Survey, Question, Read, Recite and Review.** Since I think this method is completely incorporated into the steps outlined above, I am not going to review it here. I feel it important to note, however, that it *is* incorporated, since some teachers have taken me to task for failing to mention it. (I have, however, included a more extensive discussion of SQ3R in the new edition of ***Improve Your Reading***.)

Reading technical texts

Math and science texts (or any highly technical ones, like economics) require slightly different handling. Steps 1 through 3 should still be followed, with one addition: Make sure you understand the concepts expressed in the various graphs or charts.

And do *not proceed* to step 4. You must understand one section before moving on to the next, since the next concept is usually based on the previous one. If there are sample problems, solve those that tie in with the section you have just read to make sure you understand the concepts imparted. If you still fail to grasp a key concept, equation, etc., start again and try again. But *don't* move on—you'll just be wasting your time.

These texts really require such a slow, steady approach, even one with a lot of backtracking or, for that matter, a lot of wrong turns. "Trial and error" *is* an accepted method of scientific research. The key, though, is to make it *informed* trial and error—having a clear idea of where you're heading and *learning* from each error. While trial and error is okay, it is much more important to be able to easily apply the same analysis (solution, reasoning) to a slightly different problem, which requires real understanding. Getting the right answer just because you eliminated every *wrong* one may be a very viable strategy for taking a test but it's a lousy way to assure yourself you've actually learned something.

Understanding is especially essential in any technical subjects. Yes, it's easy for some of you to do great on math tests because you have a great memory and/or are lucky and/or have an innate math "sense." Trust me, sooner or later, your luck runs out, your memory overloads and your calculations become "sense"-less. You *will* reach a point where, without understanding, you will be left confused on the shore, watching your colleagues stroke heroically off to the promised land.

It happened to me in college, where I was (*very* briefly) an electrical engineering major. As long as logarithms and integral calculus were theoretical—just remember the rules, get a little lucky and count on my built-in math "radar"—I could shine. Not only did I get a perfect 800 on the math section of the SAT, I got an 800 on the *Calculus Achievement Test* (now the SAT-II). A budding mathematical genius, *ne c'est pas?*

How to Study

Sure. Until I had to actually show I *understood* the concepts underlying all the rules and calculations, to use that understanding as the basis for practical reasoning and applying the concepts. Remember the TV show *Lost in Space*? Me during freshman year physics *and* physical chemistry. Good-bye "math sense," hello English major.

Whether math and science come easily to you or make you want to find the nearest pencil-pocketed computer nerd and throttle him, there are some ways you can do better at such technical subjects, without the world's greatest memory, a lot of luck or any "radar":

- Whenever you can, "translate" formulas and numbers into words. To test your understanding, try to put your translation into *different* words.

- Even if you're not particularly visual, pictures can often help. Try translating a particularly vexing math problem into a drawing or diagram.

- Before you even get down to solving a problem, is there any way for you to estimate the answer or, at least, to estimate the range within which the answer should fall (greater than 1, but less than 10)? This is the easy way to at least make sure you wind up in the right ballpark.

- Play around. There are often different paths to the same solution, or even equally valid solutions. If you find one, try to find others. This is a great way to increase your understanding of all the principles involved.

- When you are checking your calculations, try working *back*wards. I've found it an easier way to catch simple arithmetical errors.

- Try to figure out what is being asked, what principles are involved, what information is important, what's not. (I can't resist an example here, one that was thrown at me in 8th grade: Picture a record—the vinyl kind, before CDs. Its diameter is 9 inches. The label is perfectly centered. Its radius is 1.75 inches. The record plays at 45 revolutions per minute, and the song it plays lasts for exactly 3 minutes. The vinyl is exactly .18 mm thick. Got it? OK, here's the question: How many grooves does the record have?)

- **Teach someone else.** Trying to explain mathematical concepts to someone else will quickly pinpoint what you really know or don't know. It's virtually impossible to get someone else—especially someone who is slower than you at all this stuff—to understand if you don't!

(By the way, the answer is "one." Any *more* than one continuous groove and the song wouldn't keep playing. In case you didn't notice, *none* of the mathematical information given had the slightest bearing on the answer.)

Reading foreign language texts

Foreign language texts should be approached the same way, especially ones teaching vocabulary. If you haven't mastered the words you're supposed to in the first section, you'll have trouble reading the story in section three, even if you've learned all the words in sections two and three. Take it one step at a time and make sure you have mastered one concept, vocabulary list, lesson, before jumping ahead.

Aesthetic (pleasure) reading

> To read a writer is for me not merely to get an idea of what he says, but to go off with him, and travel in his company.
> — Andre Gide

71

How to Study

This is the kind of reading you do for pure enjoyment, for diversion, for the appreciation of a certain literary style or tone. Of course, the great works, from *Animal Farm* to *Wuthering Heights*, can also be enjoyed as pleasure reading. But if you're reading for an English or literature class, you'll probably want to combine the aesthetic method with the critical method.

Most fiction is an attempt to tell a story. There is a beginning, in which characters and setting are introduced. There is a conflict or struggle that advances the story to a climax—where the conflict is resolved. A final *denouement* or "winding up" unravels or clarifies the conclusion of the story.

Your literature class will address all of these parts using literary terms that are often more confusing than helpful. The following are brief definitions of some of the more important ones:

> *Plot:* The order or sequence of the story—how it proceeds from opening through climax. Your ability to understand and appreciate literature depends upon how well you follow the plot—the *story*.

> *Characterization:* The personalities or characters central to the story—the heroes, the heroines and the villains. You will want to identify the main characters of the story and their relationship to the struggle or conflict. Pay particular attention as to whether the characters are three-dimensional—are they real and believable?

> *Theme:* The controlling message or subject of the story, the moral or idea that the author is using the plot and characters to communicate. Some examples: man's inhumanity to man, man's impotency in his environment, the corrupting influence of power, greed and unrequited love. You need to discern this theme to really understand what it is the author wants to communicate.

Setting: The time and place in which the story takes place. This is especially important when reading a historical novel or one that takes you to another culture.

Point of View: Who is telling the story? Is it one of the central characters giving you flashbacks or a first-person perspective? Or is it a third-person narrator offering commentary and observations on the characters, the setting and the plot? This is the person who moves the story and gives it an overall tone.

The first step in reading literature is to familiarize yourself with these concepts, then try to recognize them in the novel or short story. As you begin your reading, approach it first from an aesthetic standpoint: How does it make you feel? What do you think of the characters? Do you like them? Hate them? Relate to them?

Second, make sure you know what's going on—this involves the plot or story line and the development of the characters. On a chapter-by-chapter basis, you may find it helpful to keep a sheet of paper on which you can jot a sentence or two of the plot development (and, if you wish, characters introduced, etc.). For example, your notes on the first chapter of **The Time Machine** by H. G. Wells might read:

> Time Traveller, Psychologist, the Provincial Mayor, the Medical Man, a Very Young Man and Filby are in the Time Traveller's house. It is a winter evening (fire is going). They talk about the geometry of Four Dimensions—4th dimension is time. TT declares he has discovered way to move about in Time and shows them experimental verification—small model for Time Machine (took two yrs to make) that disappears when activated. Claims it is traveling in time. Announces that big machine is nearly ready and, when finished, he will use it for a journey in Time.

I have written these notes out, but obviously you would not need to do so. Simply listing the points in outline fashion or noting key words would be sufficient. Does this adequately summarize the first chapter so you wouldn't have to read it? Not really. Yes, it tells you the characters introduced and, in bare-bones fashion, what happened.

But it leaves out all of the details of the philosophical debate that begins the book and, most importantly, cannot possibly capture the mystery, foreboding and thrill of entering an adventure that Wells manages to convey in this single chapter. And it leaves out important information like the themes carried out in the book, use of literary devices, etc.

To truly summarize this chapter, you might label the above paragraph "Plot," then include separate notes under the headings "Themes" and "Literary." This would certainly help you both understand what you've read and simplify your review task come test time.

Take out the crayolas

If you have a desk drawer full of magic markers *(a.k.a. highlighters)*, you're probably already familiar with the process of underlining text. It can be a useful method for zeroing in on what's important, both during the classroom preparation stage and when you're compiling your notes. But be careful that in your quest to highlight pertinent information, you don't end up with your entire reading assignment in yellow.

The other danger of highlighting is that you tend not to pay as much attention to what you're reading as you underline your material. If you're not comfortable reading without your yellow marker, please keep this advice in mind:

1. Underlining should identify words or sentences that capsulize a section's major ideas or themes.

2. Underlining should indicate the relative importance of things, allowing you to concentrate your review time on key words, facts and concepts (underlined)

and skip the digressions, examples and extraneous explanations (not underlined).

To sharpen your underlining skills, read though the next three paragraphs and indicate with your highlighter which information you feel is important:

> For the most part, young people entering the field do not understand just what public relations involves or how to employ public relations techniques to address a communications issue. Some think it involves just dealing with the press. Others think it is mostly writing. Still others are sure that what*ever* it is, it's involved somehow with affecting public opinion, but then confuse it with advertising.
>
> In fact, public relations might be defined in many ways. Webster's New World Dictionary defines it as "those functions of a corporation concerned with informing the public of its activities, policies, etc., and attempting to create favorable public opinion." Other texts have used slightly different definitions.
>
> We tell anyone interested in public relations that the best way to understand the field is to intern in either a public relations firm or a corporate communications department of a major company. This will give you firsthand experience and exposure to the many varied facets of public relations *before* you have to commit yourself to the field.

It should be obvious that the definition of public relations is the essence of the first two paragraphs. You'll want to remember "those functions of a corporation... favorable public opinion." Highlight that entire definition. (If this were in one of your textbooks, you may want to write in the margin "PR: def" as a way of catching your attention and moving your eye to this important information.)

Secondly, you may highlight the word "intern" or even the whole phrase "best way to understand the field is to intern," the key point in the third paragraph.

How to Study

Now if you had to review that book for a test, you would glance at two sentences—the two you highlighted—to get the gist of three paragraphs.

How fast can you understand?

> When we read too fast or too slowly, we understand nothing.
> — Pascal

Are you worried that you read too slowly? You probably shouldn't be—less-rapid readers are not necessarily less able. What counts is what you comprehend and remember. And like anything else, practice will probably increase your speed levels. If you must have a ranking, take any randomly selected text of 250 words and read it from start to finish, noting the elapsed time on your watch. Then score yourself as follows:

Under 20 seconds	Very Fast
21-30 secs.	Fast
31-45 secs.	Average
46-60 secs.	Slow
61+ secs.	Very Slow

You should only worry—and plan to do something about it—if you fall in the slow or very slow range. Unless you do, you are probably reading as fast as you need to. Again, the relationship between your reading speed and your comprehension is paramount: Read too fast and you may comprehend less; reading slowly does not necessarily mean you're not grasping the material. There are several things you can do to improve these reading mechanics.

To increase your reading speed:

1. Focus your attention and concentration.
2. Eliminate outside distractions.

3. Provide for an uncluttered, comfortable environment.

4. Don't get hung up on single words or sentences, but *do* look up (in the dictionary) key words that you must understand in order to grasp an entire concept.

5. Try to grasp overall concepts rather than attempting to understand every detail.

To increase comprehension:

1. Try to make the act of learning sequential—comprehension is built by adding new knowledge to existing knowledge.

2. Review and rethink at designated points in your reading. Test yourself to see if the import of the material is getting through.

3. If things don't add up, discard your conclusions. Go back, reread and try to find an alternate conclusion.

4. Summarize what you've read, rephrasing it in your notes, in your own words.

Most importantly, read at the speed that's comfortable for you. Though I *can* read extremely fast, I *choose* to read novels much more slowly so I can appreciate the author's word play. Likewise, any material that I find particularly difficult to grasp slows me right down. I read newspapers, popular magazines and the like very fast, seeking to grasp the information but not worrying about every detail.

Should you take some sort of speed reading course, especially if your current speed level is slow? I can't see that it could particularly hurt you in any way. I can also, however, recommend that you simply keep practicing reading, which will increase your speed naturally.

How to Study

Habits that decrease reading speed/comprehension

1. Reading aloud or moving your lips when you read.
2. Reading mechanically—using your finger to follow words, moving your head as you read.
3. Applying the wrong *kind* of reading to the material.
4. Lacking sufficient vocabulary.

Remembering what you read

In a world where the ability to master and remember a growing explosion of data is critical for individual success, too little attention is paid to the dynamics of memory and systems for improving it. Developing your memory is probably the most effective way to increase your efficiency, in reading and virtually everything else.

Retention

Retention is the process by which we keep imprints of past experiences in our minds, the "storage depot." Subject to other actions of the mind, what is retained can be recalled when needed. Things are retained in the same order in which they are learned. So your studying should build one fact, one idea, one concept upon another.

Broad concepts can be retained more easily than details. Master the generalities and the details will fall into place.

If you think something is important, you will retain it more easily. So convincing yourself that what you are studying is something you must retain (and recall) increases your chances of adding it to your storehouse.

Recall

This is the process by which we are able to bring forth those things that we have retained. Recall is subject to strengthening through the process of repetition. *Recall is least effective immediately after a first reading,* emphasizing the importance of review. The dynamics of our ability to recall are affected by several factors.

- We most easily recall those things that are of interest to us.
- Be selective in determining how much you need to recall. All information is not of equal importance—focus your attention on being able to recall the most *important* pieces of information.
- Allow yourself to react to the data you are studying. Being able to associate new information with what you already know will make it easier to recall.
- Repeat, out loud or just in your mind, what you want to remember. Find new ways of saying those things that you want to recall.
- Try to recall broad concepts rather than isolated facts.
- Use the new data you have managed to recall in a meaningful way—it will help you recall it the next time.

Recognition

This is the ability to see new material and recognize it for what it is and what it means. Familiarity is the key aspect of recognition—you will feel that you have "met" this information before, associate it with other data or circumstances and then recall the framework in which it logically fits.

If you've ever envied a friend's seemingly wondrous ability to recall facts, dates and telephone numbers virtually at will, take solace that, in most cases, *this skill is a result of study and practice,* not something anyone is born with.

There are certain fundamental memory systems that, when mastered, can significantly expand your capability. It is beyond the scope of this book to teach you these detailed techniques, but if you feel you need help, why not consult your local library? Of course, I recommend my own *Improve Your Memory,* but I'm sure you'll find a number of helpful titles at your library.

Test your reading comprehension

Remember: Comprehending what you read is, to a great extent, more important than how fast you read it. The following section will test your reading comprehension. The first selection is the easiest, the following two progressively more difficult. Read each selection carefully, then answer the questions. And note that there is not necessarily a single right answer for each question, only one closest to the truth.

Fiction (least difficult)

David approached the house slowly. An attitude of caution overcame him as without prior knowledge, just what he could expect to find was problematic. Communications with the old man and woman had been sparse and in recent years very few words of their welfare had come to the family.

Economic conditions in that part of the world were just beginning to stabilize. The first Great War and now this revolution cast a doubt on one's ability to eke out even the most meager of existences. He had come prepared with a gift of dollars, which he knew would help to guarantee their welfare.

Finally he arrived at the door and within a moment the three of them were embracing. How strange, he thought, the way the bonds of family could bridge oceans. Immediately he realized he belonged and that his long journey had indeed been the right thing to do.

Questions (choose only one answer)

1. In this account, the writer's primary purpose is to:
   A. Give the reader a view of economic conditions

B. Describe the difficulties of meeting long-lost relatives
C. Emphasize the bonds of family that remain regardless of circumstance
D. Pad the book by another page
E. Demonstrate that virtue is its own reward

2. Where is the book set?
A. Asia
B. The United States
C. Unknown
D. Not the United States
E. Heaven

3. What relation is David to the people he is visiting?
A. They are his parents
B. They are his grandparents
C. They are family friends
D. They are relatives
E. They are people he met on the Road to Morocco

History (more difficult)

Franklin Delano Roosevelt's chief accomplishments encompass both domestic and international activities.

First elected when the country suffered a severe economic collapse, he was instrumental in mobilizing the nation's people and resources to spearhead a recovery. In present-day economic terms, he presided over the greatest turnaround in modern history.

Applying the full weight of central government, he established the principle of government as the court of last resort. Specifically this welfare approach included: the establishment of Social Security; a variety of "make-work" projects that created millions of jobs; federally guaranteed insurance on depositors' bank accounts; stock market regulation; rural power and electrification; the establishment of minimum wage and working conditions standards; and unemployment insurance.

How to Study

During World War II, FDR presided over the largest military buildup and subsequent engagement ever faced by the nation. He was the successful Commander-In-Chief directing the military forces of the nation in a global encounter with the forces of Fascism.

Roosevelt, early on, recognized the threat the Axis powers presented and mobilized the country—primarily by helping to arm England via the mechanism of Lend-Lease—against them. There were those, and many in high places, who sought to minimize the American role in the impending war. Roosevelt, however, was accurate in his belief in the inevitability of U.S. involvement. He recognized the ultimate threat to American freedom that Fascism represented. When the Japanese attack on Pearl Harbor made war a fait accompli, Roosevelt was ready.

Roosevelt's wartime stewardship demonstrated, as it had during the Depression, his genius for leadership. His words mobilized the nation. His efforts, together with those of Stalin and Churchill, led the Free World to victory.

Some revisionist historians would argue that postwar activities (started at the Yalta Conference) jeopardized America's postwar influence, particularly in Eastern Europe. It seems more logical to assume the Cold War rivalry was a natural outgrowth of two antithetical systems, each feeling heady with victory, each determined to make their manner of governing the law of the land.

Roosevelt's place in history is assured. Though himself privileged by birth, he displayed an unusual compassion for the average man. A noncombatant because of his illness, he demonstrated a courage and leadership which stood as a fine example for battlefield troops.

Questions

1. The writer's main purpose in this selection is to:
   A. Describe world conditions during FDR's presidency.
   B. Demonstrate Roosevelt's grasp of both domestic and international problems.

C. Indicate that leadership is essential for an effective presidency.

D. Indicate the broad scope of programs developed to reinvigorate a depressed economy.

E. Emphasize the inevitability of confrontation between countries with different forms of government.

2. The author asserts that Roosevelt:
   A. Provided necessary leadership in turning the economy around.
   B. Did not hesitate to involve government.
   C. Was the grandfather of the welfare state.
   D. Pioneered many social reforms and make-work programs.
   E. Died too soon

3. One can conclude that Roosevelt:
   A. Understood the real threat posed by Fascism.
   B. Was able to marshal the necessary cooperation among allies for the conduct of a successful global war effort.
   C. Understood the necessity to arm England.
   D. Was not anxious for war but realistic about its possibility.
   E. None of the above.

4. The phrase "postwar influence" refers directly to:
   A. Agreement on spheres of power determined at Yalta.
   B. An acknowledgment of the military realities when hostilities ceased.
   C. The recognition of the competing natures of Democracy and Communism.
   D. A permanent division of the world along superpower lines.
   E. All of the above.

How to Study

Current events (most difficult)

The bickering that has gone on among both white and black South African dissidents, primarily over whether to boycott that country's first free elections, is reminiscent of the playground squabbles we went through as children. Bosom buddies one moment, down-in-the-dirt antagonists the next, back in class again minutes later.

Is such bickering merely a method of negotiation, a way for each of the sides, but primarily the African National Congress and the Zulu nationalists, to convince the other that unless their demands are met, they may well scuttle the entire process? Again, is it not like the child who, denied the field at first base, takes his ball and goes home, allowing pride to overcome his desire to play ball, no matter what position he is given?

Perhaps, but the real passions that lie behind such brinkmanship cannot be denied. And neither can the very real sense that for many of the "players," there is far more emotion at work than political maneuvering or logic.

Most of the citizenry is tired of the daily deadlines, the factionalism, the ever-changing alliances, enemies turning into friends overnight, friends waking up enemies. Breakthroughs are announced in newspapers' morning editions only to be proved false by the evening.

This disarray has in many cases overshadowed the active campaigning by Nelson Mandela's African National Congress and President F. W. de Klerk's National Party, the two major factions in the election. Their campaign has been further eroded by the party that has, so far at least, opted out of the elections altogether—the Zulu nationalists' Inkatha Freedom Party. It is unthinkable that they and their mercurial leader, Mangosuthu G. Buthelezi, will hold themselves out of the election process entirely. They simply have too much to lose—patronage, credibility and the ability to incorporate their own platform in the newly formed government—to boycott the elections entirely.

But Buthelezi and his party have defied logic and done the unthinkable before. While many observers believe his holdout to be a shrewd strategic move, one that will enable him to extract every possible concession before he enters the electoral fray, others remember his withdrawal from negotiations last year that many feel would have enabled him to displace de Klerk as the titular opposition leader and expand his influence beyond the predominantly Zulu province of Natal. Instead, he became even more insular and isolated, scared off many former supporters and lost the votes of many who were ready to make him the alternative to Mandela and the ANC.

Questions

1. The author believes the Inkatha Freedom Party:
   A. Can be a viable alternative to the ANC for voters
   B. Cannot afford to boycott the election process
   C. Is ready to expand beyond Natal province
   D. Should depose its leader

2. It is obvious from this reading that:
   A. It's not important who wins the game but how you play that counts
   B. Violence will continue long after the elections are over
   C. Emotions are playing as important or more important a role in South Africa's elections that political logic
   D. F. W. de Klerk cannot win a majority of the votes in this election

3. The writer's purpose in this selection is to:
   A. Discuss the current political situation in South Africa
   B. Analyze the position of the Inkatha Freedom Party
   C. Describe the bickering between the political parties
   D. All of the above

How to Study

4. The writer thinks the winner of the election will be:
   A. F. W. de Klerk and the National Party
   B. Nelson Mandela and the African National Congress
   C. Inkatha Freedom Party
   D. None of the above

Now check your answers on page 90. This is the kind of testing material you'll come upon again and again, and practice *does* make perfect. If you didn't get at least eight of these eleven questions right, work on your memory skills and start highlighting your texts as you read to make comprehension of the main points easier.

Did you have to read the entire text of each selection more than once to get the meaning? Did you find yourself reading more slowly than usual? Did it take you more than three minutes to read any of the texts?

If you answered "yes" to *any* of these questions, stop patting yourself on the back and start working on what you still need to improve—comprehension *with* speed.

Build a library

> The reading of all good books is like conversation
> with the finest men of past centuries.
> — Descartes

If you are ever to become an active, avid reader, access to books will do much to cultivate the habit. I suggest you "build" your own library. Your selections can and should reflect your own tastes and interests, but try to make them wide and varied. Include some of the classics, contemporary fiction, poetry and biography.

Save your high school and college texts—you'll be amazed at how some of the material retains its relevance. And try to read a newspaper every day to keep current and informed.

Your local librarian can refer you to any number of lists of the "Great Books," most of which are available in inexpensive paperback editions. Here are three more lists—my own—of: 1) the "great" classical authors; 2) the "great" not-so-classical authors, poets and playwrights; and 3) a selection of my own "great books."

You may want to incorporate these on your buy list, especially if you're planning a summer reading program.

(Note: I'm sure I have left off someone's favorite author or "important" title from these lists, even though I have revisited them and revised them pretty extensively. So be it. They are not meant to be comprehensive, just relatively representative. I doubt anyone would disagree that a person familiar with the majority of authors and works listed would be considered well-read!)

Some "great" classical authors

Boccaccio	Confucius	S. Johnson	Flaubert
Emerson	Kant	Spinoza	Rousseau
Aesop	Dante	Homer	Voltaire
Aquinas	Descartes	Horace	Shakespeare
Cervantes	Machiavelli	Nietzsche	Vergil
Chaucer	Goethe	Plato	Ovid
Aristotle	Dewey	Aeschylus	Santayana
J. Caesar	Erasmus	Milton	Swift
Balzac	Hegel	Montaigne	Pindar
Cicero	Aristophanes	Plutarch	Burke

Some other "great" authors

Albert Camus	Brendan Behan
Aldous Huxley	Carl Sandburg
Aleksandr I. Solzhenitsyn	Charles Dickens
Alexandre Dumas	Charles Lamb
Anthony Burgess	Charlotte Bronte
Arthur Conan Doyle	Daniel Defoe
Ayn Rand	D. H. Lawrence
Bertolt Brecht	Dorothy Parker
Bertrand Russell	Dylan Thomas

How to Study

e e cummings
E. M. Forster
Edgar Allan Poe
Edna Ferber
Edward Albee
Ellery Queen
Emile Zola
Emily Bronte
Emily Dickinson
Erich Maria Remarque
Ernest Hemingway
Eudora Welty
Eugene O'Neill
Evelyn Waugh
Ezra Pound
F. Scott Fitzgerald
Feodor Dostoevsk1
Franz Kafka
George Bernard Shaw
George Eliot
George Orwell
George Sand
Gertrude Stein
H. G. Wells
H. H. Munro (Saki)
H. L. Mencken
H. W. Longfellow
Henry Miller
Hermann Hesse
Herman Melville
Isaac Asimov
Ivan Turgenev
J. D. Salinger
J. R. R. Tolkien
James Jones
James Joyce
James Russell Lowell
James Thurber
Jean Paul Sartre
John Galsworthy
John Hersey
John Keats
John Updike
Jose Ortega y Gasset
Joseph Conrad
Joseph Heller

Leo Tolstoy
Lewis Carroll
Lillian Hellman
Lord Byron
M. M. Kaye
Marcel Proust
Mark Twain
Maxim Gorki
Nathaniel Hawthorne
Nikolai Gogol
O. Henry
Oscar Wilde
Pearl Buck
P. G. Wodehouse
Percy Bysshe Shelley
Robert Frost
Robert Heinlein
Robert Louis Stevenson
Robert Penn Warren
Rudyard Kipling
Samuel Beckett
Saul Bellow
Sherwood Anderson
Sinclair Lewis
T. S. Eliot
Tennessee Williams
Theodore Dreiser
Thomas Hardy
Thomas Mann
Thomas Wolfe
Thornton Wilder
Truman Capote
Upton Sinclair
Victor Hugo
Vladimir Nabokov
W. H. Auden
Walt Whitman
Washington Irving
W. Somerset Maugham
William Blake
William Butler Yeats
William Faulkner
William James
William Saroyan
William Styron
William Wordsworth

Some "great" works

A Farewell to Arms
A Long Day's Journey Into Night
A Portrait of the Artist as a
 Young Man
A Streetcar Named Desire
A Tale of Two Cities
The Adventures of
 Huckelberry Finn
The Adventures of Tom Sawyer
The Aeneid
Aesop's Fables
Alice In Wonderland
All Quiet On the Western Front
An American Tragedy
Animal Farm
Anna Karenina
Arrowsmith
Atlas Shrugged
As I Lay Dying
Babbitt
The Bell Jar
The Bonfire of the Vanities
Brave New World
The Brothers Karamazov
The Canterbury Tales
Catch-22
The Catcher in the Rye
Confessions of an English
 Opium Eater
The Count of Monte Cristo
Crime and Punishment
David Copperfield
Death Comes for the Archbishop
Death of a Salesman
The Deerslayer
Demian
Don Juan
Don Quixote
Ethan Fromme
Far From the Madding Crowd
The Federalist Papers
For Whom the Bell Tolls
The Foundation
The Good Earth

The Grapes of Wrath
The Great Gatsby
Gulliver's Travels
Hamlet
Heart of Darkness
The Hound of the Baskervilles
I, Claudius
The Idiot
The Iliad
The Immoralist
The Invisible Man
Jane Eyre
Julius Caesar
Kim
King Lear
Lady Chatterley's Lover
"Leaves of Grass"
The Legend of Sleepy Hollow
Les Miserables
Look Homeward, Angel
Lord Jim
The Lord of the Rings
MacBeth
The Magic Mountain
Main Street
Man and Superman
The Merchant of Venice
The Metamorphosis
Moby Dick
Mother Courage
Native Son
1984
Of Human Bondage
Of Mice and Men
The Old Man and the Sea
Oliver Twist
One Flew Over the Cuckoo's
 Nest
Othello
Our Town
"Paradise Lost"
The Pickwick Papers
The Picture of Dorian Gray
Portrait of a Lady

How to Study

Pride and Prejudice
The Prophet
"The Raven"
The Red Badge of Courage
The Remembrance of Things
    Past
The Return of the Native
"The Road Not Taken"
Robinson Crusoe
Romeo and Juliet
The Scarlet Letter
Siddhartha
Silas Marner
Sister Carrie
The Sound and the Fury

Steppenwolf
The Sun Also Rises
The Tale of Genji
Tender Is the Night
The Thin Red Line
The Time Machine
Tom Jones
The Trial
Ulysses
Vanity Fair
Walden
War and Peace
"The Wasteland"
Winesburg, Ohio
Wuthering Heights

Reading every one of these books will probably make you a better reader; it will certainly make you more well-read. That is the extra added bonus to establishing such a reading program—an appreciation of certain authors, certain books, certain cultural events and the like is what separates the cultured from the merely educated and the undereducated.

Read on and enjoy!

Read on

Insofar as one can in a single chapter, I've tried to sum up the essentials of reading. It is not a finite science but rather a skill and appreciation that one can develop over time. Good grade school training is essential. And for those of you who have been able to identify problem areas, there are always remedial classes.

Having a "love affair" with books is the best boost you can give yourself. Reading is active, not passive. To paraphrase Timothy Leary: "Turn on, tune in, read a book."

Answers to this chapter's comprehension quizzes: Fiction—1) C; 2) C; 3) D. History—1) B; 2) A; 3) A; 4) A. Current Events—1) B; 2) C; 3) D; 4) D.

Chapter Four

HOW TO ORGANIZE YOUR TIME

We all have problems with time.

We can't control it—we can't slow it down or speed it up.

We can't save it up—all we can do is decide how we're going to spend it.

We invariably need more of it...and don't know where to find it.

Then we wonder where the heck it all went.

But *time* is not really the problem. After all, it's the one "currency" that all people are given in equal supply, every day—24 hours, same for you, me and Bill Clinton. The problem is that most of us simply let too much of it slip through our fingers—because we have *never been taught how to* manage *our time*...or why we should try. Our parents never sat us down to give us a little "facts of time" talk. And time management skills aren't part of any standard academic curriculum.

How to Study

Whether you're a book author typing as fast as you can to meet the publisher's deadline, a student juggling five classes and a part-time job or a parent working, attending classes and raising a family, a simple, easy-to-follow time management system is crucial to your success. And, despite your natural inclination to proclaim that you just don't have the *time* to spend scheduling, listing and recording, it's also the best way to give yourself *more* time.

Spending time now to save more later

In this chapter, we'll develop a time management plan for an entire term, learn how to prioritize tasks and then create our daily schedules.

Identify the starting line

Like any of the skills I've already talked about in **How to Study**, you can't race off to your ultimate goal until you figure out where *your* starting line is. So the first step to overhaul your current routine is to *identify* that routine, in detail. My suggestion is to chart, in 15-minute increments, how you spend every minute of every day *right now*. While a day or two might be sufficient for some of you, I recommend you chart your activities for an entire week, including the weekend.

This is especially important if, like many people, you have huge pockets of time that seemingly disappear, but, in reality, are devoted to things like "resting" after you wake up, putting on makeup or shaving, reading the paper, waiting for transportation or driving to and from school or work. Could you use an extra hour a day, either for studying or for fun? Make better use of "dead" time and you find all the time you need.

For example, learn how to do multiple tasks at the same time. Listen to a book on tape while you're working around the house; practice vocabulary or math drills while you're driving;

have your kids, parents or roommates quiz you for an upcoming test while you're doing dishes, vacuuming or dusting; *always* carry your calendar, notebook(s), pens and a textbook with you—you can get a phenomenal amount of reading or studying done while in line at the bank, in the library, at the supermarket or on a bus or train.

Strategy Tip: Identify those items on your daily calendar, whatever their priority, that can be completed in 15 minutes or less. These are the ideal tasks to tackle at the laundromat, while waiting for a book to wind its way to your study cubicle or while standing in line anywhere.

One of the inherent advantages of a strictly observed schedule is that it saves time just by "being"—eliminating all that time so many of us waste just sitting down wondering what we should do next! (Not to mention trying to find the materials we need, deciding where we're going to study that night, how long, with whom, etc., etc., etc.) The more time management becomes a *habit*, the more *automatic* such decisions become, and the less time you waste making them.

The other huge advantage, of course, is the discipline such a strict schedule demands. Discipline is a wonderful commodity in that, as far as I've found, the more you're able to discipline *any* single aspect of your life, the easier it is to discipline all others. Just ask any writer who's confronted a blank sheet of paper and stared...for hours..."blocked" by unseen forces. Many will tell you the only way to break free is to continue sitting, day after day, trying again and again, no matter how difficult. You don't think *that* takes discipline?

Collect what you need

As you begin your planning session, make sure you have all of the information and materials you need to make a quality plan. Gather your class syllabuses, work schedule, dates of important family events, vacations or trips, other personal commitments (doctor appointments, parties) and a calendar of any extracurricular events in which you plan to participate.

Keeping track of your day-to-day activities—classes, appointments, regular daily homework assignments and daily or weekly quizzes—will be dealt with after we talk about those projects—studying for mid-terms and finals, term papers, theses—that require completion over a long period. Weeks. Maybe even months.

Creating your Project Board

There are two excellent tools you can use for your long-term planning. The first is a Project Board, which you can put on any blank wall or right above your desk. You can buy a ready-made chart at an art supply, stationery or bookstore. Or you can copy the format of the one I've included on pages 96 and 97.

How does the Project Board work? As you can see, it is just a variation on a calendar. I have set it up vertically—the months running down the left-hand side, the projects across the top. You can switch the order if you want. (Many "store-bought" charts come set up this way.)

Using your Project Board

In the case of each project, there is a key preparatory step before you can use the chart: You have to break down each general assignment into its component parts. So, for example, in the case of an English report on Dante that just got assigned, we have identified the steps as:

1. Finalize topic
2. Initial library research
3. General outline
4. Detailed library research

5. Detailed outline
6. First draft
7. Second draft
8. Check spelling and proofread
9. Get someone else to proofread
10. Type final draft
11. Proofread again
12. Turn in!

Next to each specific task, we have estimated the time we would expect to spend on it. (For more information about the steps required to writing a term paper, see Chapter 7 in this book and read **Write Papers,** another of the six companion volumes to **How to Study**.)

The more time you have to complete a project, the easier it is to procrastinate about dealing with it, even to putting off identifying the steps and working them into your regular schedule. If you find yourself leaving such long-term projects to the last week, schedule the projects furthest away—the term paper due in three months, the oral exam 10 weeks from now—*first*. Then, trick yourself—schedule the completion date at least seven days prior to the actual turn-in date, giving yourself a one-week cushion for life's inevitable surprises. (Just try to forget you've used this trick. Otherwise, you'll be like the perennial latecomer who set his watch 15 minutes fast in an effort to finally get somewhere on time. Except that he always reminded himself to add 15 minutes to the time on his wrist, defeating the whole purpose.)

The second project involves working on a team with other students from your entrepreneurship class to create a hypothetical student business. While the steps are different, you'll notice that the concept of breaking the project down into separate and manageable steps and allocating time for each doesn't change.

Sample Projects Board

MONTH/WEEK		PROJECT: STUDENT CORPORATION
1st MONTH	Week 1	Initial group meeting: Discuss overall assignment and possible products or services—bring list of three each to meeting (1 hour)
	Week 2	Finalize product or service; finalize organization of group and longterm responsibilities of each subgroup. (3)
	Week 3	Subgroup planning and short-term assignments (2)
	Week 4	Work on individual assignment from subgroup (?)
2nd MONTH	Week 1	Work on individual assignment from subgroup (?)
	Week 2	Work on individual assignment from subgroup (?)
	Week 3	Integrate individual assignment with rest of subgroup (?)
	Week 4	Meet with entire group to integrate plans (?)
3rd MONTH	Week 1	Finalize all-group plan; draft initial report (?)
	Week 2	Type and proof final report (?)
	Week 3	
	Week 4	
	DUE DATE	3RD MONTH/end of Week 2

PROJECT: DANTE TERM PAPER	REVIEW/EXAM SCHEDULE
Finalize topic (1 hour)	Review prior month's History notes (3)
Initial library research (2) General outline (1)	Review prior month's English notes (2)
Detailed library research (3) Detailed library research (3)	Review prior month's Science notes (4) Review prior month's Math notes (4)
Detailed library research (3) Detailed outline (1) First draft (4), Additional research (2)	Review 1st MONTH History notes (3) Review 1st MONTH English notes (2) Review 1st MONTH Science notes (4) Review 1st MONTH Math notes (4)
Second draft, spellcheck, proof (10) Independent proof (1) Type final draft and proof (4)	2nd MONTH History notes (3) 2nd MONTH English notes (2) 2nd MONTH Science notes (4) 2nd MONTH Math notes (4)
end of 3RD MONTH	end of 3RD MONTH

How to Study

However, because time allocation in later steps depends on what assignments you're given by the group, we have had to temporarily place question marks next to some steps. As the details of this project become clearer and specific assignments are made, your Project Board should be changed to reflect both more details and the specific time required for each step.

You should also include on your Project Board time for studying for all your final exams. If you have skipped ahead and read Chapter 8, you know that cramming for tests doesn't work very well in the short term and doesn't work at all over the long term. So you have taken my advice in that chapter and made it a habit to review your class notes on each subject on a monthly basis. You've decided that every Sunday morning is "review time" and allocated one Sunday a month to review the previous month's work in each subject.

As a result of this plan, you'll notice there is little time allocated to last-minute cramming or even studying for a specific final the week before it is given—just a couple of hours to go over any details you're still a little unsure of. While others are burning the midnight oil in the library the night before each exam, you're getting a good night's sleep and will enter the tests refreshed, relaxed and confident. As a byproduct of this study schedule, by the way, you will find that salient facts and ideas will remain with you long after anybody is testing you on them.

Keep adding any other important projects throughout the term and continue to revise it according to actual time spent as opposed to time allocated. Getting into this habit will make you more aware of how much time to allocate to future projects and make sure that the more you do so, the more accurate your estimates will be.

Using a Term Planning Calendar

The Term Planning Calendar, an example of which is shown on pages 100 and 101, can be used in concert with or in place of the Project Board. (There's a blank form on page 117.)

To use it with the Project Board, start by transferring all the information from the Project Board to your Term Planning Calendar. Then add your weekly class schedule, work schedule, family celebrations, vacations and trips, club meetings and extracurricular activities. Everything. The idea is to make sure your Calendar has *all* the scheduling information, while your Project Board contains just the briefest summary that you can ingest at a glance.

Leave your Project Board on your wall at home; carry your Term Planning Calendar with you. Whenever new projects, appointments or meetings are scheduled, add them immediately to your Calendar. Then transfer the steps involving major projects to your Project Board.

To use it in place of the Project Board, just don't make a Project Board. Put all the information—including the steps of all your projects and the approximate time you expect each to take—right on the Calendar.

It's up to you which way to go. Personally, I prefer using *both,* for one simple reason: I like being able to look at the wall and see the entire term at a glance. I find it much easier to see how everything fits together this way than by trying to "glance" at a dozen different weekly calendars or even three monthly ones.

I also find it difficult to see which steps go with which projects without studying the calendar (although I admit color-coding would solve the problem), whereas the very set-up of the Project Board makes such information easy to glean.

High school students may find it quite easy to use only the calendar, as they are usually not subject to quite as many long-term projects as college or graduate students. But once you're in college, especially if you have more than an average number of papers, reports, projects, etc., you'll find the Project Board a very helpful extra tool.

Month	Mon	Tue	Wed	Thu	Fri	Sat	Sun
← Feb	18	19	20	21	22	23	24
→ March →	25	26	27 conference 4-5	28	1	2	3
	4	5	6	7	8 Afternoon: A.A.P. meeting	9	10
	11 Sociology Presentation	12	13 Math: Ch.1-3	14	15	16	17 Trip Home
	18	19	20 Math: Ch.4	21	22	23	24

Month	Mon	Tue	Wed	Thu	Fri	Sat	Sun
	25	26	27 Math: Ch.5	28	29	30	31
April	1	2	3 No Math Due	4	5	6 Trip to Jim & Dana's	7
	8	9	10 Math: Ch. 6-8	11	12 Sociology Paper due!	13	14
	15 Biology Lab Journal Due!!	16 Last day of class	17	18	19	20 Biology Final 3:00	21
	22 Math Final 2:00	23	24	25	26 ☺	27	28

← CAMPING !!! →

101

Planning your days and weeks

Now that you've got the "big picture"—the term—under control, it's time to learn about tools that will help you organize your days and weeks.

For any time-management system to work, it has to be used continually. Make an appointment with yourself at the end of each week—Sunday night is perfect—to sit down and plan for the following week. This may just be the best time you spend all week, because you will reap the benefits of it throughout the week and beyond.

Step 1: Make a "to do" list

First, you must identify everything you need to do *this week*. Look at your Project Board and/or Term Planning Calendar to determine what tasks need to be completed this week for all your major school projects. Add any other tasks that must be done this week: from sending off a birthday present to your sister to attending your monthly volunteer meeting to completing homework that may have just been assigned.

Once you have created your list, you can move on to the next step, putting your tasks in order of importance.

Step 2: Prioritize your tasks

When you sit down to study without a plan, you just dive into the first project that comes to mind. Of course, there's no guarantee that the first thing that comes to mind will be the most important. The point of the weekly Priority Task Sheet is to help you arrange your tasks *in order of importance*. That way, even if you find yourself without enough time for everything, you can at least finish those assignments that are most important. A completed sample is on page 103; a blank form for you to photocopy is on page 118.

Priority Rating	Scheduled?	**Priority Tasks This Week** Week of 3/28 through 4/3
		Sociology Paper
H		— Library Search
M		— Outline
L		— Rough Draft
		Math Assignments
H		— Ch. 4
M		— Ch. 5
M		— study for test

How to Study

First, ask yourself this question, "If I only got a few things done this week, what would I want them to be?" Mark these high-priority tasks with an "H." After you have identified the "urgent" items, consider those that are *least* important—items which could wait until the following week to be done, if necessary. You may have tasks that you consider very important, but don't have to be completed this week. These items might be less important this week, but are likely to be rated higher next week. Mark these low-priority items with an "L."

Strategy Tip: If you push aside the same low-priority item day after day, week after week, at some point you should just stop and decide whether it's something you need to do at all! This is a strategic way to make a task or problem "disappear." In the business world, some managers purposefully avoid confronting a number of problems, waiting to see which will simply solve themselves through benign neglect. If it works in business, it can work for you in school.

All other items fit somewhere between the critical tasks and those of low priority. Review the remaining items, and if you're sure none of them are either "H" or "L," mark them with an "M" (for middle priority).

Some students have told me they like to do their priority list on 3 x 5 cards, for the same reason I like them for note-taking—they're easy to sort, move, change. I find them too cumbersome in this case, but some of you may want to try it.

Step 3: Fill in your Daily Schedule

Before you start adding papers, projects, homework, study time, etc., to your calendar, fill in the "givens"—the time you need to sleep, eat, work, attend class. Even if your current routine consists of meals on the run and sleep wherever you find it, build the assumption *right into your schedule* that you are going to get eight hours of sleep and three decent meals a day. You may surprise yourself and find that there is still enough time to do everything you need. (Though we all know someone who sleeps three hours a night, eats nothing but junk and still finds a way to get straight As, most experts would contend that regular, healthy eating and a decent sleep schedule are key attributes to any successful study system.)

Now transfer the items on your Priority Task Sheet to your Daily Schedule forms. (See page 107 for a sample completed Schedule, page 119 for a form you can photocopy.) Put in the "H" items first, followed by the "M" items. Then, fit in as many of the "L" items that you still have room for.

By following this procedure, you'll make sure you give the amount of time needed to your most important priorities. You can devote your most productive study times to your most important tasks, and plug in your lower priorities as they fit.

Besides the importance of the task and the available time you have to complete it, other factors will determine how you fit your Daily Schedules together. Some will be beyond your control: work schedules, appointments with professors, counselors, doctors. But there are plenty of factors you *do* control, which you should consider as you put together your Daily Schedules for the week.

Schedule enough time for the task but, particularly when working on long-term projects, not so much time that you "burn out." Every individual is different, but most students study best for blocks of about one and a half to three hours, depending on the subject. You might find history fascinating and be able to read for hours. Calculus, on the other hand, may be a subject that you can best handle in "small bites," a half-hour to an hour at a time.

Don't overdo it. Plan your study time in blocks, breaking up work time with short leisure activities. It's helpful to add these to your schedule as well. You'll find that these breaks help you think more clearly and creatively when you get back to studying.

Even if you tend to like longer blocks of study time, be careful about scheduling study "marathons"—a six- or eight-hour stretch rather than a series of two-hour sessions. The longer the period you schedule, the more likely you'll have to fight the demons of procrastination. Convincing yourself that you are really studying your heart out, you'll also find it easier to justify time-wasting distractions, scheduling longer breaks, and, before long, quitting before you should.

Use your Daily Schedule *daily*

Each night (or in the morning before the day begins) look at your schedule for the upcoming day. How much free time is there? Are there "surprise" tasks that are not on your schedule but need to be? Are there conflicts you were not aware of at the beginning of the week? By checking your Daily Schedule *daily,* you'll be able to respond to these changes.

Strategy Tip: Get into the habit of getting ready for the next day before you go to bed the night before. Believe me, it's an absolutely fantastic feeling to *start* the day completely organized...especially if you oversleep!

Using these tools effectively

There are thinkers and there are doers.

Then there are those who think a lot about doing.

Organizing your life requires you to actually *use* the Project Board, Term Planning Calendar, Priority Task Sheets and Daily Schedules. Once you have discovered habits and patterns of study that work for you, continue to use and hone them. Be flexible enough to add new techniques you learn and alter schedules that circumstances have made obsolete.

Be realistic

Plan according to *your* schedule, *your* goals and *your* aptitudes, not some ephemeral "standard." Allocate the time you

Daily Schedule

date: **3/30**

Assignments Due		Schedule
Bio. Lab work.	5	
Math, Ch. 4	6	
	7	
	8	
	9	Biology
To Do/Errands	10	Sociology
Call Erin — 871-4031	11	↓ ↓
Books to library	12	Lunch w/ Kim
☑ Bank	1	read:
☐ Groceries	2	Ch.5 (Soc.)
Drop by Jim's	3	Math class
	4	TRAVEL
	5	
Homework	6	Math homework
1) Math Ch.5 1-9	7	work on paper
2) Sociology paper	8	
(rough draft)	9	
	10	
	11	
	12	

expect a project to take *you*, not the time it might take someone else, how long your teacher says it should take, etc. There will be tasks you accomplish far faster than anyone else, others that take you much longer.

Set priorities

Try to be realistic and honest with yourself when determining those things that require more effort, those that come easier to you. Refer back to the list of classes you like and dislike or do best and worst in. This will affect the time you need to allocate to specific projects.

Whenever possible, schedule pleasurable activities *after* study time. They will then act as incentives, not distractions.

Be flexible

No calendar is an island. Any new assignment affects whatever you've already scheduled. If you have a reasonably light schedule when a new assignment suddenly appears, it can just be plugged right into your calendar and finished as scheduled. But if you've already scheduled virtually every hour for the next two weeks, *any* addition may force you to change a whole day's plan. Be flexible and be ready. It'll happen.

Monitor and adjust

No plan of action is foolproof, so monitor your progress at reasonable periods and make changes where necessary. Remember, this is *your* study regimen—you conceived it, you can change it. You may have allocated insufficient time to one assignment, too much to another. Fallen sick, run off for an unscheduled ski weekend or received an unexpected assignment.

I know you'll be anxious to stick to your schedule, to get things done. But taking a break and sitting back to survey the landscape of your efforts provides a good check and balance against costly mistakes and omissions. And don't forget to include the breaks you need, based on your answers in Chapter 1, in your allocation of study time.

If you find that you are consistently allotting more time than necessary to a specific chore—giving yourself one hour to review your English notes every Sunday but finishing in 45 minutes or less—change your future schedule accordingly. You may use the extra 15 minutes for a task that consistently takes *longer* than you've anticipated or, if such doesn't exist, quit 15 minutes early.

Be prepared

As assignments are entered on your calendar, make sure you also enter items needed—texts, other books you have to buy, borrow or get from the library, special materials (drawing pad, magic markers, graph paper, etc.).

Nothing's worse than sitting down to do that assignment you've put off for weeks...and realizing that though *you're* finally ready to get to work, your supplies *aren't*. Have your study materials available when you need them.

Everything's relative

Like time. Car trips take longer if you have to schedule frequent stops for gas, food, necessities; longer still if you start out during rush hour. Likewise, libraries are more crowded at certain times of the day or year, which will affect how fast you can get books you need, etc. So take the time of day into account. And if your schedule involves working with others, take *their* sense of time into account. You may find you need to schedule "waiting time" for a chronically late friend...and make sure you always have a book to read with you.

Be creative

You may decide that color-coding your calendar—red for assignments that must be accomplished that week, blue for steps in longer-term assignments, yellow for personal time and appointments, green for classes—makes it easier to tell at a glance what you need to do and when you need to do it.

Once you've gotten used to your class schedule, you may decide to eliminate classes from your calendar and make it less complicated.

Adapt these tools to your own use. Try anything you think may work—use it if does, discard it if it doesn't.

One thing at a time

Accomplish one task before going on to the next one—don't skip around. If you ever stuffed envelopes for a political candidate, for example, you've probably already learned that it is far quicker and easier to sign 100 letters, then stuff them into envelopes, then seal and stamp them than to sign, stuff, seal and stamp one letter at a time.

Do your least favorite chores (study assignments, projects, whatever) first—you'll feel better having gotten them out of the way! And plan how to accomplish them as meticulously as possible. That will get rid of them even faster.

Pizza, anyone?

If you see that you are moving along faster than you anticipated on one task or project sequence, there is absolutely nothing wrong with continuing onto the next part of that assignment or the next project step. The alternative, of course, is to say *yea!*, forget the next assignment, finish early and buy a pizza. There's nothing wrong with the latter approach.

If you are behind, don't panic. Just take the time to reorganize your schedule and find the time you need to make up. You may be able to free up time from another task or put one part of a long-term project off for a day or two. And if such rescheduling means canceling a date or missing your favorite TV show, then it's up to you to decide which comes first.

Don't try to remember

All of the tools we've discussed and the various other hints should get you into the habit of writing things down. Amazingly you'll find that not having to remember all these items will free up space in your brain for the things you need to concentrate on or *do* have to remember. As a general rule, write down the so-called little things and you'll avoid data overload and clutter.

But don't forget!

As a time management axiom puts it, "Don't respond to the urgent and forget the important." It's easy to become distracted when the phone rings, your baby brother chooses to trash your room or you realize your favorite TV show is coming on. But don't just drop your books and run off.

Take a few seconds to make sure you have reached a logical stopping point. If you haven't, get back to work. If you have, jot down a note to yourself of exactly where you left off and/or anything you want to remember after your break. Then you can enjoy your break without anxiety.

Don't do it twice

Some assignments—reading a novel, taking notes from a number of library books, etc.—can be interrupted at almost any time without causing a problem. Others may consist of a number of related steps, but you may still be able to pause after any step.

But beware of those time-consuming and complicated tasks that, once begun, demand to be completed. Taking notes from a number of books might be a task you can accomplish in half a dozen sittings, but reviewing and organizing them to outline your report definitely requires your undivided attention from start to finish. Interrupting at any point might mean starting all over again. What a waste of time *that* would be!

How to Study

If you're writing and have a brainstorm—just as the phone rings (and you know it's from that person you've been waiting to hear from all week)—take a minute to at least jot down your ideas before you stop. Inspiration does not always drop in twice the same night. If you let yourself lose your "train of thought," you may find yourself alone at the station, watching your train chug off into the night.

Someone always knows better

Single out one or two fellow students—preferably with better grades—and compare notes. Not class notes, *study* notes—find out what's working for somebody else and try to incorporate these techniques into your own program.

Keep daydreams in their place

Nothing can be as counterproductive as losing your concentration, especially at critical times. Learn to ward off those enemies that would alter your course and you will find your journey much smoother.

Interruptions come in two distinct varieties: the unconscious and the conscious. The former include those distractions in your own mind that prevent clear and concentrated thinking—your fantasies and daydreams. Give in to these demons, lose your concentration, and you will find hours happily drifting by. Unfortunately, when you get to the end of the day, you will find you have accomplished nothing on your list. Trust me: The depression from falling behind will not be assuaged by the glow of your fantasies!

Know your study clock

One way to guard against these mental intrusions is to know your own study clock and plan your study time accordingly. Each of us is predisposed to function most efficiently at specific times of the day (or night). Find out what sort of study clock you are on and schedule your work during this period. (Most people's peak activity hours fall during the mid-day period. There is a notable reduction of productive hours starting with late afternoon.)

This is not a foolproof solution, however. Even if you're always on schedule, have every material you need and organized your calendar with more colors than a box of Crayolas, you may find yourself staring out the window and dreaming of (choose one) a boy, a girl, a night, a weekend, a trip, an adventure, a TV show, a fantasy, or just the way the sun reflects in the pond. Life is like that. So what do you do?

(1) Banish those thoughts as fast and furiously as Salem handled witches. Shorten the scheduled time before your next break and, when you take that break, enjoy it! Then go back to work. If it continues happening, take more frequent breaks or just keep plugging away. Like anything else, concentration is a learned skill, one in which practice *does* make perfect.

(2) Say the heck with it and take a break right away. If your schedule is loose enough, give yourself an hour, the morning or even the rest of the day off. Fantasize to your heart's content (or, even better, go out and *do* something about the fantasies), then go back to studying with a mind ready to concentrate on the task at hand.

Neither one of these solutions is always right. There are times to fight the dreams and there are days to say the heck with it and go to a ball game, the mall, a movie, whatever.

Put Ma Bell on hold

The second category of intrusions are conscious acts or activities. Beware of uninvited guests and *all* phone calls: Unless you are ready to take a break, they will only get you off schedule.

More subtle enemies include the sudden desire to sharpen every pencil in the house, an unheard-of urge to clean your room, an offer to do your sister's homework. Anything, in other words, to avoid your own work. If you find yourself doing any-thing *but* your work, either take a break then and there or pull yourself together and get down to work. Self-discipline, too, is a learned habit that gets easier with practice.

The simple act of saying "no!" (to others or to yourself) will help insulate yourself from these unnecessary (and certainly postponable) interruptions. Remember, what you are seeking to achieve is not just time—but *quality* time. Put your "do not disturb" sign up and stick to your guns, no matter what the temptation.

Reward yourself

In line with my advice above, there *are* times to ignore the schedule, pat yourself on the back and take off and lie on the grass. But why wait until the siren call of interruption forces you to waste precious time fighting for concentration—especially if you wind up just giving in anyway? Why not in-corporate "reward time" into your regular schedule?

Depending on your schedule, of course, this could mean a night off every week to do something you like, a weekend a month, etc. Alternatively, each day (if you really need help, each *hour)* you could simply set up a reward as an incentive for finishing an assignment, a project, a day's work, whatever.

Rewards do not necessarily require large amounts of cash, long trips or other people. The more frequently you run into trouble concentrating on the task at hand, the more frequently you should create some incentive to help yourself: "If I get this next thing done, I'll take off 15 minutes and have an ice cream." Then enjoy the whole banana split!

A special note for commuters

If you live at home (as opposed to being housed on cam-pus), there are some special pressures with which you need to be ready to contend:

Your commute to school will probably be longer than if you could roll out of bed and walk to class. It will certainly require more wakefulness, even if you just have to stumble to a subway or bus (but especially if you have to drive!). You'll also have travel time problems if you need to use the library after you've returned home or, for that matter, need to return to the campus for any reason. It's especially important *you* minimize your travel time, planning enough to maximize your use of the campus facilities without scheduling a trip home in between.

While nobody likes walking to class in rain, sleet or snow—except, perhaps, future postal employees—it is invariably easier to walk a few tree-lined blocks than drive a few miles in inclement weather. Take weather problems into account when scheduling your commute.

The very act of living at home—whether as a child or one "married with children"—brings with it responsibilities to others you could minimize living in a dorm. Be ready to allocate time to these responsibilities and include them in your study schedule. They're as inevitable if you live at home as meat loaf on Tuesdays.

Now comes the payoff

Once you start using your Project Board, Term Planning Calendar, Priority Task Sheets and Daily Schedules, you will reap the benefits every day.

Anything—even school—seems less overwhelming when you have it broken into "bite-size" pieces...and you already know the flavor.

You no longer worry about when you'll get that paper done—you've already planned for it.

You'll accomplish it all—one step at a time.

My time management program allows for flexibility. In fact, I encourage you to adapt any of my recommendations to

How to Study

your own unique needs. That means it will work for you whether you are living in a dorm, sharing an apartment or house with roommates, or living with a spouse and children. You *can* learn how to balance school, work, fun, and even family obligations.

As you get used to managing your time, planning ahead as well as planning your week and even your days, you'll quickly discover that you seem to have more time than ever before.

(Please feel free to photocopy the blank forms on pages 117 to 119 and use them in your own time management system.)

Term Planning Calendar

Fill in due dates for assignments and papers, dates of tests, and important non-academic activities and events

Month	Mon	Tue	Wed	Thu	Fri	Sat	Sun

117

How to Study

Priority Rating	Scheduled?	**Priority Tasks This Week**
		Week of _____ *through* _____

Daily Schedule

date:

Assignments Due

Schedule

	5
	6
	7
	8
	9

To Do/Errands

	10
	11
	12
	1
	2
	3
	4
	5

Homework

	6
	7
	8
	9
	10
	11
	12

Chapter Five

HOW TO EXCEL IN CLASS

Whatever your grade level, whatever your grades, whatever your major, whatever your ultimate career goals, we all have one thing in common: the classroom experience.

Most teachers utilize the classroom setting as an opportunity to embellish and interpret material covered in the text and other assigned readings. If you always complete your reading assignments before class, you'll be able to devote your classroom time to the "add-on" angles the teacher will undoubtedly cover.

You've got to have class

Exactly how you'll use the skills we'll cover in this chapter will be influenced by two factors: the type of classroom set-up and the particular methods and styles employed by each of your teachers.

Each of the following general class formats will require adjustments to accomplish the above goals:

Lectures: Podium pleasantries

Teacher speaks, students listen. Pure lectures are quite common from the college level up, but exist only rarely at the high school level. Lecture halls at larger colleges may fill up with hundreds of students for some of the more popular courses.
Primary Emphases: Listening; note taking.

Discussions: Time to speak your mind

Also called *tutorials* or *seminars,* discussion groups are again common on the college level, often as adjuncts to courses boasting particularly large enrollments. A typical weekly schedule for such a course might consist of two lectures and one or more discussion groups. Often led by graduate teaching assistants, these discussion groups are much smaller—usually no larger than two dozen students—and give you the chance to discuss points made in the lecture and material from the text and other assigned reading.

Such groups rarely follow a precise text or format and may wander wildly from topic to topic, once again pointing out the need for a general mastery of the course material, the "jumping-off" point for discussion.
Primary Emphases: Asking / answering questions; analyzing concepts and ideas; taking part in discussion.

Combination: Best (or worst) of both

Some post-secondary courses are, for want of a better term, *combination classes*; that is, they combine the lecture and discussion formats (pretty much the typical kind of pre-college class you're used to). The teacher prepares a lesson plan of material he or she wants covered in a specific class. Through lecture, discussion, question and answer, audio-visual presentations or a combination of one or more such devices, the material is covered.

Your preparation for this type of class will depend to a great extent on the approach of each individual instructor. Such classes also occur on the post-secondary level—college, graduate school, trade school—when class size is too small for a formal lecture approach.

Primary Emphases: Note taking; listening; participation; asking and answering questions.

Hands-on: Getting your hands dirty

Hands-on classes, including science labs and various vocational education courses (industrial arts, graphics, etc.), occur at all levels, from high school up.

They are concerned almost exclusively with *doing* something—completing a particular experiment, working on a project, etc. The teacher may demonstrate certain things before letting the students work on their own, but the primary emphasis is on the student carrying out his or her own projects while in class.

On the college level, science labs are merely overseen by graduate assistants. Trade schools may use a combination of short lectures and demonstrations and hands-on workshops—you can't become a good auto mechanic just by reading a book on cleaning a distributor.

Primary Emphasis: Development and application of particular manual and technical skills

Rarely can a single class be neatly pigeonholed into one of these formats, though virtually all will be primarily one or another. It would seem that size is a key factor in choosing a format, but you can't always assume, for example, that a large lecture course, filled with 200 or more students, will feature a professor standing behind a rostrum reading from his prepared text. Or that a small class of a dozen people will tend to be all discussion.

During my college years, for example, I had a Religion teacher who, though his class was one of the more popular on campus and regularly drew 300 or more students to each session, rarely lectured at all. One never knew *what* to expect when entering his classroom. One week it would be a series of musical improvisations from a local jazz band, with a variety of graduate assistants talking about out-of-body (religious, note the tie-in) experiences. Another session would consist entirely of the professor arguing with a single student over one key topic...which had *nothing* to do with that week's (or any *other* week's) assignment.

In another class of merely 20 students, the professor teaching us physical chemistry would march in at the sound of the bell and, without acknowledging anyone's presence or saying a word, walk to the blackboard and start writing equations, which he would continue to do, working his way across the massive board, until, some 20 or 30 minutes later, he ran off the right side. Slowly, he would walk back to the left side...and start writing all over again. He never asked questions. Never asked *for* questions. In fact, I'm not sure I remember him uttering *any*thing for three solid months!

Know your teacher

What is also extremely important for you to know and understand is the kind of teacher you've got and his or her likes, dislikes, preferences, style and what he or she expects you to get out of the class. Depending on your analysis of your teacher's habits, goals and tendencies, preparation may vary quite a bit, whatever the chosen format.

Some teachers are very confident fielding questions at any point during a lesson; others prefer questions to be held until the end of the day's lesson; still others, and my chemistry prof is a good example, discourage questions (or any interaction for that matter) entirely. Learn when and how your teacher likes to field questions and ask them accordingly.

No matter how ready a class is to enter into a freewheeling discussion, some teachers fear losing control and veering away from their very specific lesson plan. Such teachers may well encourage discussion but always try to steer it into the set path they've decided upon. Other teachers thrive on chaos, in which case you can never be sure just what's going to happen.

Approaching a class with the former teacher should lead you to participate as much as possible in the class discussion, but warn you to stay within whatever boundaries he or she has obviously set.

Getting ready for a class taught by the latter kind of teacher requires much more than just reading the text—there will be a lot of emphasis on your understanding key concepts, interpretation, analysis and your ability to apply those lessons to cases never mentioned in your text at all!

Some teachers' lesson plans or lectures are, at worst, a review of what's in the text and, at best, a review plus some discussion of sticky points or areas he or she feels may give you problems. Others use the text or other assignments merely as a jumping-off point—their lectures or lesson plans might cover numerous points that aren't in your text at all. Preparing for the latter kind of class will require much more than rote memorization of facts and figures—you'll have to be ready to give examples, explain concepts in context and more.

Most of your teachers and professors will probably have the same goals: to teach you how to think, learn important facts and principles of the specific subject they teach and, perhaps, how to apply them in your own way.

In classes like math or science, your ability to apply what you've learned to specific problems is paramount.

Others, like your English teacher, will require you to analyze and interpret various works, but may emphasize the "correct" interpretation, too.

Whatever situation you find yourself in—and you may well have one or more of each of the above "types"—you will need to adapt the skills we will cover in this chapter to each situation.

How to prepare for *any* class

In general, here's how you should plan to prepare for any class before you walk through the door and take your seat:

Complete all assignments

Regardless of a particular teacher's style or the classroom format he or she is using, virtually every course you take will have a formal text (or two or three or more) assigned to it. Though the way the text explains or covers particular topics may differ substantially from your teacher's approach to the same material, your text is still the basis of the course and a key ingredient in your studying. You *must* read it, plus any other assigned books, *before* you get to class.

You may sometimes feel you can get away without reading assigned books beforehand, especially in a lecture format where you *know* the chance of being called on is slim to none. But fear of being questioned on the material is certainly not the only reason I stress reading the material that's been assigned. You will be lost if the professor decides—for the first time ever!—to spend the entire period asking *the students* questions. I've had it happen. And it was *not* a pleasant experience for the unprepared.

You'll also find it harder to take clear and concise notes because you won't know what's in the text (in which case you'll be frantically taking notes on material you could have underlined in your books the night before, if you had read them, of course) or be able to evaluate important vs. unimportant information.

If you're heading for a discussion group, how can you participate without your reading as a basis? I think the lousiest feeling in the world is sitting in a classroom knowing that, sooner or later, you are going to be called on and that you don't know the material.

Remember: This includes not just reading the main text but any other books, articles, etc., previously assigned, plus handouts that may have been previously passed out. It also means completing any nonreading assignments—turning in a lab report, preparing a list of topics or being ready to present your oral report.

Review your notes

Both from your reading and from the previous class. Your teacher is probably going to start this lecture or discussion from the point he or she left off last time. And you probably won't remember where that point was from week to week...unless you check your notes.

Have questions ready

As discussed in Chapter 3, preparing questions as you read text material is an important step. Here's your chance to find the answers to the questions that are still puzzling you. Go over your questions before class. That way, you'll be able to check off the ones the lecturer or teacher answers along the way and only ask those left unanswered.

Prepare required materials

Including your notebook, text, pens or pencils and other such basics, plus particular class requirements like a calculator, drawing paper or other books.

Before we get into how to take notes, it's important to talk about how to set up your notebook(s). There are a variety of ways you can organize your note-taking system:

1. Get one big two- or three-ring binder (probably three or more inches thick) that will be used for all notes from all classes. This will require a hole punch, "tab" dividers and a healthy supply of pre-punched paper.

You can divide the binder into separate sections for each course/class, in each of which you will keep notes from your lectures and discussion groups, reading lists, assignment deadlines and any course handouts—all material set up in chronological fashion. Alternatively, you can further subdivide each section into separate sections for reading notes, class notes and handouts.

This system is widely used, especially in high school, but it has two key disadvantages: First, holes that constantly tear, requiring that you patiently paste on those reinforcing circles, a boring and time-wasting task. And second, woe unto ye that lose your binders, for within it is everything ye cherish, and surely ye shall wallow in a sea of incompletes for the rest of your days.

The former problem can be solved by using either a spring-operated binding mechanism—which requires no holes at all, let alone "reinforcements"—or a multi-pocket file folder in which weekly or daily notes can be stapled together and filed along with handouts, assignments, etc.

The latter problem can be solved by selectively "culling" your notebook every week (perhaps at the same time at which you plan the upcoming week?) so, at worst, you lose a week's worth of material, not an entire semester's.

2. Use one of the above systems but get smaller binders, one for each course/class (with the same options regarding the type of binder and how to protect yourself from losing all your notes—if only from a single class).

3. Use separate notebooks (they're a lot lighter than binders) for notes, both from your reading and class. Use file folders for each class to keep handouts, project notes and copies, etc. They can be kept in an accordion file or in a multi-pocketed folder.

Whichever system you choose—one of the above or an ingenious one of your own—do *not* use the note card system for preparing papers and oral reports you will learn in Chapter 7. While it's my all-time favorite system for that application, it does *not* work well for class note-taking...and I've tried it.

Prepare your attitude

Don't discount the importance of the way you approach each class mentally—getting the most out of school in general and any class in particular depends in good measure on how ready you are to really take part in the process. You must be "up" for school, "up" for each class. It is *not* sufficient, even if you're otherwise well-prepared, to just sit back and absorb the information. Learning requires your active participation every step of the way.

What to do in class

Keep in mind your own preferences and under what circumstances you do best—refer back to the first two chapters and review your skills lists. You'll need to concentrate hardest on those courses in which you do most poorly, no matter what the style of the teacher.

Sit near the front. You should make distraction as difficult as possible by sitting as close to the instructor as you can.

You've probably realized by now that the farther you sit from the teacher, the more difficult it is to listen. Sitting toward the back of the room means more heads bobbing around in front of you, more students staring out the window...and encouraging you to do the same.

Sitting up front has several benefits. You will make a terrific first impression on the instructor since you might very well be the only student taking a seat in the front row. He'll see immediately that you have come to class to listen and learn, not just take up space.

You'll be able to hear the instructor's voice clearly, and the instructor will be able to hear *you* clearly.

Finally, being able to see the teacher clearly will help ensure that your eyes don't wander around the room and out the windows, taking your brain with them. If you have the option of picking your seat, head right for the head of the class(room).

Avoid distracting classmates. The gum cracker. The doodler. The practical jokester. The whisperer. Even the perfume sprayer. Your fellow classmates may be kind and thoughtful friends, entertaining lunch companions and great fun at parties, but their little quirks, idiosyncrasies and personal hygiene habits can prove distracting when you sit next to them in class. Knuckle-cracking and note-passing are just some of the evils that can divert your attention in the middle of your biology professor's discourse on bivalves. Avoid them.

Sit up straight. Do I sound like your mother? I know you don't want to hear it, but for once she's right. To listen effectively, you must sit correctly, in a way that will let you stay comfortable and relatively still during the entire lecture. If parts of your body start to ache or fall asleep, your attention will inevitably wander. "The mind can retain only as much as the bottom can sustain."

Listen for verbal clues

Identifying note-worthy material means finding a way to separate the wheat—that which you should write down—from the chaff—that which you should ignore. How do you do that? By *listening* for verbal clues and *watching* for the nonverbal ones.

Certainly not all teachers will give you the clues you're seeking. But many will invariably signal important material in the way they present it—pausing (waiting for all the pens to rise), repeating the same point (perhaps even one already made and repeated in your textbook), slowing down their normally supersonic lecture speed, speaking more loudly (or more softly), even by simply stating, "I think the following is important."

There are also a number of words that should *signal* note-worthy material (and, at the same time, give you the clues you need to logically organize those notes at the same time): "First of all," "Most importantly," "Therefore," "As a result," "To summarize," "On the other hand," "On the contrary," "The following (number of) reasons (causes, effects, decisions, facts, etc.)."

These (and similar words and phrases I'm sure you can think of yourself) give you the clues to not just write down the material that follows but to put it in context—to make a list ("First," "The following reasons"); establish a cause-and-effect relationship ("Therefore," "As a result"); establish opposites or alternatives ("On the other hand," "On the contrary"); signify a conclusion ("Therefore," "To summarize"); or offer an explanation or definition.

And watch for nonverbal clues

Studies have shown that only a fraction of communications is carried in the words themselves. A great deal of the message we receive when someone is speaking to us comes from body language, facial expression and tone of voice.

Most instructors will go off on tangents of varying relevance to the subject matter. Some of these will be important, but, at least during your first few lessons with that particular teacher, you won't know which.

Body language can be your clue.

If the teacher begins looking at the window or his eyes glaze over, he's sending you a clear signal: "Put your pen down. This isn't going to be on any test."

On the other hand, if he turns to write something down on the blackboard, makes eye contact with several students and/or gestures dramatically, he's sending an even clearer signal about the importance of the point he's making.

Of course, there are exceptions to this rule. There was a trigonometry professor I endured who would get most worked up about the damage being done to the nation's sidewalks by the deadly menace of chewing gum.

Ask questions

No, don't raise your hand to ask or answer questions every 90 seconds. Being an active listener means asking *yourself* if you understand everything that has been discussed. If the answer is "no," ask the instructor questions at an appropriate time or write down questions that you must have answered to understand the subject fully.

Challenge yourself to draw conclusions from the things that the instructor is saying. Don't just sit there letting your hand take notes. Let your mind do something, too. Think about the subject matter, how it relates to what you've been assigned to read and other facts you've been exposed to.

To tape or not to tape

I am opposed to using a tape recorder as a substitute for an active brain in class for the following reasons:

- *It is time-consuming.* To be cynical about it, not only will you have to waste time sitting in class, you'll have to waste more time listening to that class *again!*

How to Study

- *It is virtually useless for review.* Rewinding and fast-forwarding through cassettes to find the salient points of a lecture can be torture. During the hectic days before an exam, are you going to want to waste time listening to a lecture when you can read so much more quickly?

- *It offers no back-up.* Only the most diligent students will record *and* take notes. What happens if your tape recorder malfunctions? How useful will blank or distorted tapes be when it's time to review? If you're going to take notes as a back-up, why not just do a good job note-taking and save the time and effort of listening to that lecture again?

- *It costs money.* Compare the price of blank paper and a pen to that of a recorder, batteries and tapes. The cost of batteries *alone* should convince you that you're better off going the low-tech route. (Save those batteries for your Walkman.)

- *You miss those "live" clues* we discussed earlier when you rely on your tape-recorded lecture for garnering notes. When all you have is a tape of your lecture, you don't see that zealous flash in your teacher's eyes, the passionate arm-flailing, the stern set of the jaw, all of which should scream, "Listen up. This will be on your test!"

Having said all this against tape recorders and note-taking, I concede that there are situations in which tape recorders can be useful—such as when your head is so stuffed up with a cold that "active listening" during an hour-long lecture is virtually impossible. With this exception noted, I still maintain that a tape recorder is no substitute for good listening skills.

What is "chaff" anyway?

Taking concise, clear notes is first and foremost the practice of discrimination—developing your ability to separate the essential from the superfluous, the key concepts, key facts, key ideas from all the rest. In turn, this requires the ability to listen to what your teacher is saying and copying down only what you need to in order to understand the concept. For some, that could mean a single sentence. For others, a detailed example will be the key.

Just remember: The quality of your notes usually has little to do with their *length*—three key lines that reveal the core concepts of a whole lecture are far more valuable than paragraphs of less important data.

So why do some people keep trying to take verbatim notes, convinced that the more pages they cover with scribbles the better students they're being? It's probably a sign of insecurity—they haven't read the material and/or don't have a clue about what's being discussed, but at least they'll have complete notes!

Even if you find yourself wandering helplessly in the lecturer's wake, so unsure of what she's saying that you can't begin to separate the important, note-worthy material from the nonessential verbiage, use the techniques discussed in this chapter to organize and condense your notes anyway.

If you really find yourself so lost that you are just wasting your time, consider adding a review session to your schedule (to read or reread the appropriate texts) and, if the lecture or class is available again at another time, attend again. Yes, it *is*, strictly speaking, a waste of your precious study time, but *not* if it's the only way to learn and understand important material.

Understand the big picture

If you are actively listening, and listening before you write, then your understanding of the "big picture" ought to follow naturally. Let's say your history teacher is rattling off dates and names of battles. Your note-passing classmate in the back may go into a panic as he scrambles to jot down all the tongue-twisting foreign names that she's shooting off faster than a machine gun.

But *you*, who are sitting up front and listening actively, pause with pen in hand as your teacher sums up her point: that battle activity increased to a frenzy in the final months before the war's end. You jot down a brief note to that effect, knowing that you can check your textbook for all the names, dates and details of specific battles.

Your poor friend in the back, while capturing most of the battle names, missed the main point, the big picture, and now will feel compelled to memorize the list of names and dates, even though he doesn't know why he copied them down in the first place.

Tkng grt nts in clss

You *know* the first line of the Gettysburg address. You know the formula for Einstein's theory of relativity. You know what date Pearl Harbor was bombed. So why waste time and space writing these facts down?

Frequently, your teacher presents material that is commonly known in order to set the stage for further discussion or to introduce material that is more difficult. Don't be so conditioned to slavishly copy dates, vocabulary, terms and names that you mindlessly scribble down information you already know.

Tailor your note-taking to class format

The extent of note-taking required—as well as the importance of those notes to your success in class—will depend largely on the format of the class. In a lecture, for example, your teacher might not even know your name. Consequently, your note-taking and listening skills are all you will have in your quest for top grades.

Seminars or discussion groups place a great deal of emphasis on how skillfully you both ask and answer questions. But you should not neglect taking notes. Be all ears while the discussion is flowing, but, as soon as possible after class, write down the most important points discussed.

In hands-on classes, such as science and language labs, art classes and courses in industrial skills, keep a notebook handy in case something comes up that you think you should remember for an exam. I had a chemistry teacher who, during labs, quite often launched into extensive discussions on theory. The less dull-witted among us quickly learned to keep our notebooks close by, capturing facts and figures he never mentioned in class...but did on the exams!

Develop your shorthand skills

You don't have to be a master of shorthand to streamline your note-taking. Here are five ways:

1. Eliminate vowels. As a sign that was ubiquitous in the New York City subways used to proclaim, "If u cn rd ths, u cn gt a gd jb." (If you can read this, you can get a good job.)

2. Use word beginnings ("rep" for representative, "con" for congressperson) and other easy-to-remember abbreviations.

3. Stop putting periods after all abbreviations (they add up!)

4. Use standard symbols in place of words. Here is a list that will help you out in most of your classes (you may recognize many of these symbols from math and logic):

≈	*Approximately*
w/	*With*
w/o	*Without*
wh/	*Which*
→	*Resulting in*
←	*As a result of / consequence of*
+	*And or also*
*	*Most importantly*
cf	*Compare; in comparison; in relation to*
ff	*Following*
<	*Less than*
>	*More than*
=	*The same as, equal to*
↑	*Increasing*
↓	*Decreasing*
esp	*Especially*
△	*Change*
⊂	*It follows that*
∴	*Therefore*
∵	*Because*

5. Create your own symbols and abbreviations based on your needs and comfort-level.

There are two specific symbols I think you'll want to create—they'll be needed again and again:

Ⓦ   That's my symbol for *"What?,"* as in "What the heck does that mean", "What did she say?" or "What happened? I'm completely lost!" It denotes *something* that's been missed—leave space in your notes to fill in the missing part of the puzzle after class.

(M) That's my symbol for "My idea" or "My thought." I want to clearly separate my own thoughts during a lecture from the professor's— put in too many of your own ideas (without noting that they *are* yours) and your notes begin to lose some serious value!

Feel free to use your own code for these two important instances; you certainly don't have to use mine.

While I recommend using all the "common" symbols and abbreviations listed previously *all* the time, in *every* class, in order to maintain consistency, you may want to create specific symbols or abbreviations for each class. In chemistry, for example, "TD" may stand for thermodynamics, "K" for the Kinetic Theory of Gases (but don't mix it up with the "K" for Kelvin). In history, "GW" is the Father of our country, "ABE" is Mr. Honesty, "FR" could be French Revolution (or "freedom rider"), "IR", the Industrial Revolution.

How do you keep everything straight? No matter what, summarize your abbreviations on each class's notes, perhaps on the front page in a corner. If you're a little more adventurous, create a list on the first page of that class's notebook or binder section for the abbreviations and symbols you intend to use regularly through the semester.

Expanding on your "shorthand"

While you're listening to your instructor, you should be thinking about what you write down. Lectures are filled with so many words that will not be at all helpful when you sit down to study for the big exam. Writing *those* words down and missing some of the truly important points of the lecture is counterproductive: Your notes may look impressively complete, but what are they completely full of? All the important stuff or...?

How to Study

For instance, if your teacher says, "The harsh terms of the Treaty of Versailles and the ineffectiveness of the Weimar Republic were two of the most prevalent themes in the early speeches of Hitler," you could write down something like:

> Erly Hitler speeches: *hrsh Versailles Trty, Wmr wknss.

If the Treaty of Versailles is something that has been discussed frequently in class, you might just write "Vrs." Continue to abbreviate *more* as more terms become readily recognizable—in that way, the speed and effectiveness of your note-taking will increase as the school year grinds on.

I've also noticed that many students are prone to write *big* when they are writing fast and to use only a portion of the width of their paper. I guess they figure that turning over pages quickly means they are taking great notes. All it really means is that they are taking notes that will be difficult to read or use when it's review time. Force yourself to write small and take advantage of the entire width of your note paper.

Now, let's look at a sample lecture so you can practice your newly developed skills.

Hitting all the right notes

Here is part of a lecture that was one of my favorites in college. It is about the comic novel. I've numbered the paragraphs here so that they can be referred to easily later on.

The Comic Perspective In Comic Novels

1 The comic perspective is one which finds its most successful expression in a presentation of contrasting methods of viewing the world. These could be categorized as that of the cynic and that of the saint. The laughter and the sense of irony that a

comic work of literature can instill in its readers is a result of the clash between these methods of seeing the world.

2   If the work of literature is to be considered at all successful, its readers will surely find themselves beset with the task of sorting among the alternatives offered by the idealistic and realistic sensibilities embodied within the characters and/or the narrative voice.

3   The comic novel is one which, at last, must leave its readers experiencing its world in the way a child experiences hers: with wonder, honesty, imagination and confusion.

4   If we conduct an overview of protagonists in great comic novels, we find characters who are very much like children. They are innocent, idealistic and often naive. Moreover, authors of the great comic novels go to great lengths to deny their characters a detailed past. It is almost as if the protagonists are born fully grown into the world of the novel.

5   We can learn very few biographical details about Don Quixote. We are told only that he has filled his head with the ideals and dreams of chivalry through his incessant reading of romantic literature. Moving ahead to Dickens, we find in The Pickwick Papers a protagonist that the author continually denies a past. It is as if, for Dickens, the intrusion or even the introduction of the past into the present must inevitably bring with it a diminution of integrity and self-sufficiency. In fact, the only instance of Mr. Pickwick attempting to remember his past results in the protagonist falling asleep before he can do so.

6   When we get to the 20th-century comic novels we notice a continuity of this device. Paul Pennyfeather is delivered into the chaotic world of Decline and Fall as if from a womb. Evelyn Waugh devotes three sentences to the history of his protagonist. He

is an orphan (someone who by definition cannot know his past) who "lived in Onslow Square with his guardian, who was abysmally bored by his company..."

While you don't have the luxury of being able to *hear* these words as you would in a real lecture, pretend that you were suddenly stripped of the benefits afforded by the printed page—the ability to reread a portion of a lecture that you wouldn't be able to "rehear."

What would you come up with? How many of the actual words from the lecture would turn up in your notes? Would you be trying to get down everything the professor said?

While this lecture *sounds* eloquent, it has more sizzle to it than steak. Hence, your notes can be quite brief. Here are what mine looked like (with the paragraph references added):

Cmc Prspctv in Cmc Nvls

1. CP=2 wys 2 C wrld—cynic, saint. Clash=lftr
2. Chrctrs, nrrtr embdy idlsm or rlsm
3. Rdr xprnc=chld's wrld view=cnfused, inncnt
4. Prtgnsts like chldrn—no past
5. eg Dkns/Pkwk, Cvnts/DonQ
6. eg Wgh/Pnnyftr

It isn't pretty, but it works

Trying to capture the eloquence and missing half of the teacher's points would make much less sense. And note that very little effort has been put into this "shorthand" approach—a few symbols (=, eg), a couple of obvious substitutions (2 for two, C for see) and the omission of most vowels. Yet it is organized, understandable and took a minimum of time to write down.

What taking such brief notes will do is allow you to sit back, listen and watch the instructor. This will help you capture the entire *message* that he or she is communicating, not just the *words*. If you think that the words are very important, try to elaborate on your shorthand while the professor's words are still rattling around in your head—right after the lecture. It's not a bad idea to do this anyway, especially as you start to develop your own note-taking shorthand. It'll allow you to make sure you understand your own abbreviations.

But is it good for you?

Do you think this sort of shorthand will work for you? You probably won't at first. When I worked as a reporter, I found that I couldn't trust my notes, at least not in the beginning. But in trying to write so much down I also discovered that I couldn't trust my note-*taking*. As I gained more experience, my note-taking became more and more productive.

Just be careful—in your fervor to adopt my shorthand system, don't abbreviate so much that your notes are absolutely unintelligible to you almost as soon as you write them!

The point here is, you must come up with a note-taking shorthand system that makes sense to *you*. You may certainly choose to abbreviate less, to write a little more. Whatever system you develop, just make sure it serves the right purpose: giving you the time to really *listen* to your instructors, rather than writing down only what they say.

Draw your way to good grades

The one problem with this whole note-taking system I've discussed is that many people find it more difficult to remember words rather than pictures, especially those who, on the "My Ideal Study Environment" chart in Chapter 2, claimed they received information best visually rather than orally.

Problem solved: ***Mapping*** is another way to take notes that stresses a more visual style—drawing or diagramming your notes rather than just writing them down.

Let me show you how to map the first few pages of this chapter as an example. Start with a clean sheet of paper and, boxed or circled in the center, write the main topic:

> How to excel in class

How do you want your picture to read—top to bottom, bottom to top, clockwise in a circle, counterclockwise? I'm going to set mine up clockwise, starting at the top (12 o'clock). After deciding on the first major topic ("Utilizing skills depends on class format") and placing it on your map, add the detail:

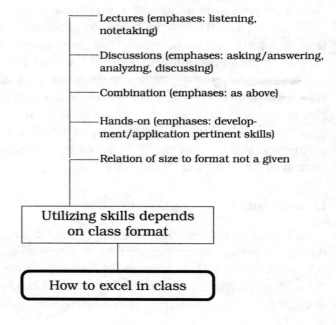

The second major topic ("Know your teacher") and those that follow take their place in the circle you've chosen in the direction you've chosen. I've completed a map containing four major topics on page 144.

Wallflowers do not get straight "A"s

In many nonlecture classes, you will find that discussion, mostly in the form of questions and answers, is actively encouraged. This dialogue serves to both confirm your knowledge and comprehension of specific subject matter and identify those areas in which you need work.

Whatever the format in which you find yourself, participate in any discussion to the best of your ability. Most teachers consider class participation a key ingredient in the grades they mete out. No matter how many papers and tests you ace, if you never open your mouth in class, you may be surprised (but shouldn't be) to get less than an "A."

If you are having trouble following a particular line of thought or argument, ask for a review or for clarification.

Don't ask questions or make points looking to impress your teacher—your real motive will probably be pretty obvious. Remember what you *are* there for—to learn the material and master it.

Based on the professor's preferences and the class set-up, ask the questions you feel need answers.

Be careful you don't innocently distract yourself from practicing your now-excellent note-taking skills by either starting to analyze something you don't understand or, worse, creating mental arguments because you disagree with something your teacher or a classmate said. Taking the time to mentally frame an elaborate question is equally distracting. All three cause the same problem: *You're not listening!*

How to Study

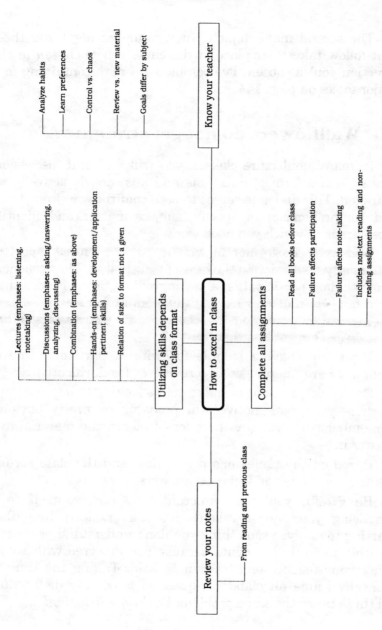

How to excel in class

Know your teacher
- Analyze habits
- Learn preferences
- Control vs. chaos
- Review vs. new material
- Goals differ by subject

Utilizing skills depends on class format
- Lectures (emphases: listening, notetaking)
- Discussions (emphases: asking/answering, analyzing, discussing)
- Combination (emphases: as above)
- Hands-on (emphases: development/application pertinent skills)
- Relation of size to format not a given

Complete all assignments
- Read all books before class
- Failure affects participation
- Failure affects note-taking
- Includes non-text reading and non-reading assignments

Review your notes
- From reading and previous class

Finally, listen closely to the words of your classmates. Knowledge has no boundaries, and you'll often find their comments, attitudes and opinions as helpful and insightful as your instructor's.

What if you're shy or just get numb whenever you're called on? Ask a question rather than taking part in the discussion—it's easier and, over time, may help you break the ice and jump into the discussion. If you really can't open your mouth without running a fever, consider a remedial course, like Dale Carnegie.

Most importantly, prepare and practice. Fear of standing in front of a class or even of participating from the safety of your seat is, for many of you, really a symptom of lack of confidence.

And *lack of confidence stems from lack of preparation.* The more prepared you are—if you know the material backwards and forwards—the more likely you will be able, even *want,* to raise your hand and "strut your stuff." Practicing with friends, parents or relatives may also help.

If you are having trouble with oral reports, they are covered separately in Chapter 7. I think you'll find the hints I've included there will eliminate a lot of the fear such talks seem to engender.

What to do *after* class

As soon as possible after your class, review your notes, fill in the "blanks," mark down questions you need to research in your text or ask during the next class, and remember to mark any new assignments on your weekly calendar.

I tend to discourage recopying your notes as a general practice, since I believe it's more important to work on taking good notes the first time around and not wasting the time it takes to recopy. *But* if you tend to write fast and illegibly, it might also be a good time to rewrite your notes so they're readable, taking the opportunity to summarize as you go. The better your notes, the better your chance of capturing and recalling the pertinent material.

It is not easy for most high school students to do so, but in college, where you have a greater say in scheduling your classes, this is why I recommend "one period on, one off"—an open period, even a half hour, after each class to review that class's notes and prepare for the next one.

Chapter Six

HOW TO USE YOUR LIBRARY

Libraries contain the written record of Humankind's brief stay on Planet Earth. They stand unparalleled as one of our finest accomplishments, unchallenged as a reference and research source. In your attempt to develop lifelong study skills, you will find yourself using this resource constantly. The library presents a single well from which we can draw knowledge and material throughout our lifetimes...without ever worrying about coming up dry.

Libraries are a staple in cities large and small across the country and represent an amazingly democratic aspect of our culture. Rules and restrictions vary from library to library—public vs. college, large vs. small—but high school and college students usually have access to virtually all library materials. And remember: These services are *free*. A library card is your ticket to the world of knowledge that could keep you busy for the rest of your life.

147

How to Study

Where to find a library

Start with your local phone directory. I can virtually guarantee there is a library within minutes of your home, since there are more than 15,000 public and nearly 5,000 academic (high school, college, university and graduate school) libraries in the United States. These are the ones you would most likely be using.

If for some reason you don't think the resources of these nearly 20,000 libraries are sufficient, there are also nearly 500 libraries on military bases throughout the country, plus over 10,000 government and special (law, medical, religious, art, etc.) libraries nationwide.

Many major university libraries dwarf all but the largest public library systems. Harvard, Yale, Princeton and similar bastions of learning offer tremendous resources even the major public libraries can't. If you have access to a major university library, consider it your good fortune and take advantage of it.

How libraries work

Most libraries are divided into reading rooms, restricted collections and unrestricted book stacks. Unrestricted book stacks are those through which anyone using the library can wander, choosing books to use while in the library or, if allowed, to take home. Restricted areas generally include any special collections of rare books, those open only to scholars or to those with particular credentials, either by library rule or by order of whoever donated the collection (and, often, the room housing it) to the library. In some libraries, *all* book stacks are closed, and *all* books must be obtained from a librarian.

Most libraries contain both *circulating materials*—those books and other items you may check out and take home with you—and *noncirculating material*—those that must be used only in the library. All fiction, general nonfiction and even most "scholarly" titles will usually be found in the first group.

Reference material, periodicals and books in special collections are usually in the second.

A look at a major library

How extensive is the collection of information at a major institution like the New York Public Library?

You'd be amazed.

Let's look only at the main library on Fifth Avenue, which stands like a monument at the dividing line between the East and West sides of Manhattan.

The first thing you discover is that no books can be taken out of this building. Since there are 82 branches throughout the five boroughs of New York (which together house more than 13 million volumes) that *will* let you take out many of their holdings, this is not exactly a problem.

So you can't take anything with you. What can you study while you're there? In addition to an extensive collection of the fiction and nonfiction works you'd expect to find in such a library, shelves of books on every conceivable topic from Airplanes to Zoology, back issues of more periodicals than you could probably name and more recordings than your local record store stocks, there are separate rooms—that's right, *rooms* (and large ones, too!)—for prints and photographs, art, microfilm, U.S. and local history and genealogy, rare books, manuscripts, archives, maps, a Science and Technology Research Center, Economic and Public Affairs Center, Slavonic and Oriental Divisions. (In the system as a whole, there's also an extensive Afro-American collection and a separate Library for the Blind and Physically Handicapped.) While a few of the more specialized collections (rare books, manuscripts, prints and photographs) require a special card just to enter the collection, most of the rest of this amazing storehouse of knowledge is open to the public!

But the NYPL also demonstrates through its many programs that the library is much more than just a repository for books. It offers a daily program of films, lectures, book discussion groups, plays, poetry readings, concerts and exhibits for adults, films, story telling and pre-school programs for children, and is a meeting place for a wide variety of community, consumer, educational, health, social service, religious and cultural groups.

You could live at the NYPL and *never* get bored!

What about *your* library?

What? You don't live in New York? And you doubt your local library can compete?

You'd be surprised at how wrong you probably are. I live in Hawthorne, New Jersey, a small suburban community. My local library—the Louis Bay IInd Library, officially—is probably typical of the kind of library you'll be working in. So a look at my library should help you appreciate what you can do at yours.

Its collection includes more than 70,000 books, current and back issues of nearly 200 magazines and newspapers, plus a variety of other material: microfiche, microfilm, compact discs, audio cassettes, phonograph records, videotapes, plus children's books and audio tapes, filmstrips and videocassettes. Not unimpressive, but a mere *one two-hundredth* of the collection available at the NYPL.

Ah, but remember the wonders the computer hath wrought. Through a work-sharing program with the library of Fair Lawn, the community next door, you can sit in the Hawthorne library and search on-line through Fair Lawn's collection of books—another 150,000 volumes. And if you need other periodicals, you have computer access to a list of the 1,500 titles in the nearby Fairleigh Dickinson University library, any of which you can obtain by FAX in minutes.

You can sit at a computer terminal in Hawthorne and access the more than six million volumes at Princeton University's Firestone Library, the second largest library in the New

York Metropolitan area (after the New York Public Library) and larger than any other public library in the nation (except for the gargantuan Library of Congress, which is a special case).

Right now, by networking with other libraries, my Hawthorne librarian could track down virtually any book, magazine, newspaper, phonograph record, audio or video cassette you want if given a reasonable amount of time.

Don't be surprised if within our lifetimes—and I left Teenland some years ago—even the smallest libraries will boast computer terminals that will enable you to call up any book or periodical in any other library...in the world. (For those of you participating in the "information superhighway" via the Internet, the future is already at hand.)

How your library is organized

To provide organization and facilitate access, most libraries utilize the Dewey Decimal Classification System, which uses numbers from 000 to 999 to classify all material by subject matter. It begins by organizing all books into 10 major groupings:

000 - 099	General	500 - 599	Science
100 - 199	Philosophy	600 - 699	Useful Arts
200 - 299	Religion	700 - 799	Fine Arts
300 - 399	Social Sciences	800 - 899	Literature
400 - 499	Language	900 - 999	History

Given the millions of books available in major libraries, just dividing them into these 10 groups would still make it quite difficult to find a specific title. So each of the 10 major groupings is further divided into 10 and each of these now one hundred groups is assigned to more specific subjects within each large group. For example, within the Philosophy classification (100), 150 is psychology and 170 is ethics. Within the

151

history classification (900), 910 is travel and 930 is ancient history.

There is even further subdivision. Mathematics is given its own number in the 500 (Science) series—510. But specific subjects within mathematics are further classified: 511 is arithmetic; 512, algebra, and so on.

Finally, to simplify your task even more, the last two digits in the Dewey code signify the type of book:

01	Philosophy of
02	Outlines of
03	Dictionary of
04	Essays about
05	Periodicals on
06	Society transactions and proceedings
07	Study or teaching of
08	Collections
09	History of

If your library doesn't use the Dewey system, it probably is organized according to the Library of Congress System, which uses letters instead of numbers to denote major categories:

A	General works (encyclopedias and other reference)
B	Philosophy, Psychology and Religion
C	History: Auxiliary sciences (archeology, genealogy, etc.)
D	History: General, non-American
E	American history (general)
F	American history (local)
G	Geography/Anthropology
H	Social sciences (sociology, business, economics)
J	Political sciences
K	Law
L	Education
M	Music
N	Fine arts (art and architecture)

P   Language/Literature
Q   Sciences
R   Medicine
S   Agriculture
T   Technology
U   Military science
V   Naval science
Z   Bibliography/Library science

There are more than 50,000 new books published each year, and your library probably buys a number of these. Books arrive almost daily and are sent to the cataloging section for classification, special bindings (if needed) and shelf placement. Once entered into the system, books are indexed in the card catalog (or, as is more and more often the case, in the computer) by author, title and subject matter. Finding a biography of Tolstoy, for example, is as easy as looking up Tolstoy in the card catalog and copying down the appropriate codes for the particular one you want (yes, your library probably has more than one!).

In a closed-shelf environment, you would give the appropriate numbers to a librarian and the books would be delivered to you. If the shelves are open, you have merely to learn the way they are organized and go search after your own books. Open-shelf areas are often designated by letters of the alphabet (for fiction), by subject matter (in smaller libraries), or, in virtually all major libraries, according to the Dewey or Library of Congress classification codes.

You may go to your local library and not even find a card catalog, which might confuse you. Am I out of touch? Hopelessly antiquated? Computers are taking over the world of business, so it's no surprise that a record-intensive "business" like the library is in the forefront of computerization. Librarians I've spoken to estimate that by the year 2000—barely five years from now—95 percent of all U.S. libraries will be "on line"—with "user friendly" computer terminals replacing old-fashioned catalog cards. Roughly 50 percent of all libraries—maybe yours—already *are* on line.

Computers also mean more things you can do. For example, at the New York Public Library, there are Apple microcomputers offering more than 100 programs, from practice math problems to SAT preparation and, of course, computer games, at more than 30 locations.

Where to start

Still feeling overwhelmed by the stacks of volumes, classification systems, card catalogs and computers? You still have no excuse for not taking advantage of your library. All you have to do—if you're at all confused about tracking down the information you need—is ask the librarian.

As a matter of fact, even if you consider yourself something of a library expert, always ask your librarian for help! Make the "information" desk at the library a regular hangout. Tell the librarians what you're working on. They will know the best sources of information for your particular topic. Consult with your librarian throughout your research. You'll find information faster. And you'll get the most out of your library.

Beyond the encyclopedia

When you were younger, you probably relied solely on the encyclopedias in your school library when you had to write a report. If you're working on a paper, even if it's for graduate school, you may still want to read encyclopedias to get a general overview of your topic. But you need to turn to other sources for more detailed information. You should read books written by experts in the field you're researching. You should read magazine and newspaper articles about your subject.

And don't stop there! Pamphlets, brochures, government documents, specialized anthologies, films and videos—these are just some of the other possible sources of information you can use for paper-writing, research, enhancing your text reading and preparing for oral reports.

Where to look for materials

You should review as wide a variety of reference materials as possible.

But how do you find out whether anyone has written a magazine or newspaper article about your topic? How do you know if there are any government documents or pamphlets that might be of help? How do you locate those written-by-the-experts reference books?

You look in your library's publication indexes. These indexes list all of the articles, books and other materials that have been published and/or are available in your library.

I've listed some of the major publication indexes below. There are many, many others, so remember to ask your librarian for additional suggestions.

1. *The Card Catalog:* This is a list of all the books in your library. (Although many libraries now store it on computer, it's still often called a card catalog because it used to be kept on index cards.) Books are indexed in three different ways: by subject, by author and by title.

2. *Newspaper Indexes:* Several large-city newspapers provide an indexed list of all articles they have published.

3. *Periodical Indexes:* To find out if any magazine articles have been published on your subject, go to a periodical index. *The Readers' Guide to Periodical Literature,* which indexes articles published in the most popular American magazines, may be one with which you're familiar.

4. **Vertical File:** Here's where you'll find pamphlets and brochures.

5. **U.S. Documents Monthly Catalog:** Useful for locating government publications.

Other resources

When you're searching for hard-to-find information, you also may want to check the following:

1. **Special Anthologies, Almanacs and Encyclopedias:** Providing more in-depth information than general encyclopedias, these are entire series devoted exclusively to specific topics.

2. **Association Directories:** An association or organization related to your topic can be one of your most valuable sources of information. Often, such organizations have a historian who can provide you with extensive literature—or, better yet, the names of experts you might interview! You can find their names and addresses here.

Many libraries print a list of its resources and a map of where they can be found. What if yours doesn't? That's right...you ask your librarian for help.

Your approach to research

All of us who have become familiar with the wonders of the library have probably developed our own approach to enjoying them and using them most efficiently. My own experience emphasizes what may be the obvious: Getting the right start is all-important. Since I try to keep from being overwhelmed with material, I start any research working with the broadest outlines or topics (and the broadest resources) and wind my way down the ladder, getting more and more specific in topic and sources as I go.

Let's assume, for example, that you have to prepare a report on the latest attempts to combat apartheid and fit this effort into a historical perspective. Here's how you might approach the task:

1. **Go to a dictionary** and look up the term apartheid. Make certain you have a firm understanding of what this word means before you proceed any further!

2. Consult any one of the numerous leading **encyclopedias** you will find in your library—Britannica, Americana, Collier's, World Book, etc. Here you'll find an overview and historical prospective on the subject of these special racial laws. Encyclopedic entries are usually the most comprehensive and concise you will find. They cover so much territory and are so (relatively) up to date that they are an ideal "big-picture" resource.

3. With overview in hand, you can start consulting the **major indexes and directories** your library has to develop a list of more specific resources. Obviously, the entries in these major resources can then be directly consulted—specific issues of *The New York Times* on microfilm, periodicals at the periodicals desk, etc. And, of course, your card catalog or computer terminal will spew out listings for hundreds of other books on the general issue of apartheid or any related subject it touches (which you learned about while skimming pertinent sections of the above general resources)—The African National Congress, Nelson and Winnie Mandela, Prime Minister Botha, black homelands, Archbishop Desmond Tutu, etc.

How to Study

In one brief tour of your library's resources, you'll easily discover and know how to obtain more material than you would need to write a book on apartheid, let alone a report.

What if you're uncomfortable in the library? An infrequent user? Or simply find it a confusing place that's more trouble than it's worth?

As I've emphasized, developing *any* habit is just a matter of practice. The more you use the library, the more comfortable you will become using it. And, of course, the more books you will become comfortable with. In a very short time, you will have your own "personal" list of resources that you start with whenever you receive an assignment.

If you want the library to become like a second home, its every shelf a familiar friend, why not go to work there? Many libraries, smaller ones in particular, often offer opportunities for paid and volunteer work. Even if you work for free, this is an excellent way to learn the ins and outs of your library.

Many of you might not use the library as much as you should (or even would like) because it's just a confusing series of catacombs. The more comfortable you are—the more you know about the materials it contains and how to locate and use them—the more you will *want* to be there.

And the more help you will be able to obtain from this great resource that's just waiting to welcome you!

Chapter Seven

HOW TO WRITE BETTER PAPERS

Trust me. It's going to happen. Whether you like it or not. Sooner or later, you'll have to prepare written and/or oral reports for virtually every one of your classes. And if you're like most students, your reaction will be the same every time: "Why me? What do I do? Where do I start?"

I'm not going to pretend that reading this chapter will make you such a good writer that you can quit school and start visiting bookstores to preen in front of the window displays featuring your latest best seller.

But there is absolutely no reason to fear a written paper or oral report—once you know the simple steps to take and rules to follow to complete it satisfactorily. Once you realize that 90-percent of preparing a paper has *nothing* to do with writing...or even being *able* to write. And once you're confident that preparing papers by following my suggestions will probably get you a grade or two higher than you've gotten before...even if you are the world's poorest excuse for a writer.

Five basic rules of paper-writing

Let's start with the fundamental rules that need to be emblazoned on your wall:

1. *Always* follow your teacher's directions to the letter.
2. *Always* hand in your paper on time.
3. *Always* hand in a clean and clear copy of your paper.
4. *Never* allow a single spelling or grammatical error in your papers.
5. *Always* keep at least one copy of every paper you write.

You wanted it *type*written?

Your teacher's directions may include:

- A general subject area from which topics should be chosen—"some aspect of Kennedy's presidency," "an 18th-century invention," "a short story by Edgar Allan Poe," etc.

- Specific requirements regarding format—typed, double-spaced, include title page, do not include title page, etc.

- Suggested length—10-15 typewritten pages.

- Other requirements—turn in general outline before topic is approved; get verbal okay on topic before proceeding; don't include quotes (from other works) longer than a single paragraph; other idiosyncrasies of your own teachers.

Whatever his or her directions, *follow them to the letter.* High school teachers may be somewhat forgiving, but I have known college professors who simply refused to accept a paper that was not prepared as they instructed—and gave the poor but wiser student an "F" for it (without even *reading* it).

If you are unsure of a specific requirement or if the suggested area of topics is unclear, it is *your* responsibility to talk to your teacher and clarify whatever points are confusing you.

It is also not a bad idea to choose two or three topics you'd like to write about and seek his or her preliminary approval if the assignment seems particularly vague.

So then my dog chewed the paper...

Since you've studied and memorized Chapter 4, there is certainly no reason, short of catastrophic illness or life-threatening emergency, for you to *ever* be late with an assignment. Barring those, there is rarely an acceptable excuse for being late. Again, some teachers will refuse to accept a paper that is late. At best, they will do so but mark you down for your lateness, perhaps turning an "A" paper into a "B"...or worse.

Is that jelly stain worth a "B"?

Teachers have to read a lot of papers and shouldn't be faulted for being human if, after hundreds of pages, they come upon your jelly-stained, pencil-written tome and get a bit discouraged. Nor should you be surprised if they give you a lower grade than the content might merit just because the presentation is so poor.

I am not advocating that you emphasize form over substance. Far from it—the content is what the teacher is looking for, and he or she will primarily be basing your grade on *what* you write. But presentation is important. So follow these simple rules:

- Never handwrite your paper.
- If you're using a word processor or word-processing program on your computer, use a new ribbon in your dot matrix printer and/or check the toner cartridge of your laser printer. If you type (or have someone else type) your paper, use clean white bond and (preferably) a new carbon ribbon so that the images are crisp and clear.
- Unless otherwise instructed, always double space a typewritten paper.
- Use a simple typeface that is clear and easy-to-read; avoid those that are too big—stretching a five-page paper to 10—or too small and hard to read.
- And never use a fancy italic, modern or any other ornate or hard-to-read typeface for the entire paper.

Can your old papers speak?

There should be a number of helpful messages in your returned papers, which is why it's so important to retain them. What did your teacher have to say? Are there comments applicable to the paper you're writing now—poor writing, lack of organization, lack of research, bad transitions between paragraphs, poor grammar or punctuation, misspellings? The more such comments—and, one would expect, the lower the grade—the more extensive the "map" your teacher has given you for your *next* paper, showing you right where to "locate" your "A".

If you got a low grade but there aren't any comments, shouldn't you have asked the teacher why you got such a poor grade? You may get the comments you need to make the next paper better. You will also be showing the teacher you actually care, which could help your grade the next time around.

Three! Three! Three jobs in one!

As you tackle your assignment, you actually have three different jobs ahead of you:

1. *You must search for information.* First, you will dig up all the facts you can about the subject. You will gather statistics, historical data, first-person accounts and other information. You will read reference books, newspaper stories, magazine articles, scholarly journals and other materials. You may watch a relevant video or film, even interview a live expert or two.

   As you do all of this, your role is like that of a *reporter*. Your job is to find out the truth. You must gather data with an unbiased eye. You can't discard or ignore information that doesn't fit in with your personal opinions or expectations.

2. *You must analyze the data.* Once you have gathered information, you must study all the data—again, from an objective viewpoint. Like a scientist evaluating the results of an experiment, you must review the evidence and decide what it means. You must draw a conclusion about your subject.

3. *You must report your findings.* Finally, you must share your new-found knowledge. You will write an in-depth report, and tell your readers what you have learned.

The Fry paper-writing system

The more complex a task or the longer you need to complete it, the more important your organization becomes. By breaking down any paper-writing project into a series of manageable steps, you'll start to feel less chaotic, hectic and scared right away.

How to Study

Here are the steps that, with some minor variations along the way, are common to virtually any written report or paper:

1. Finalize your topic
2. Carry out initial library research
3. Prepare a general outline
4. Do detailed library research
5. Prepare detailed outline (from note cards)
6. Write your first draft
7. Do additional research (if necessary)
8. Write your second draft
9. Spell-check and proofread
10. Have someone *else* proofread
11. Produce a final draft
12. Proofread one last time
13. Turn it in and collect your "A"

Create a work schedule

Get out your calendar. Find the date on which your paper is due. How many weeks till then? Plan to spend half of that time on research, the other half on writing.

Now, block out set periods of time during each week to work on your paper. Schedule two- or three-hour chunks of work time, rather than many short periods.

As you make up your work schedule, set deadlines for completing various steps of your paper. Look at the example on page 165.

Of course, I can't tell you exactly how much time to set aside, because I don't know the specifics of your paper or your work speed. I *can* tell you that you should plan on consulting and/or taking notes from at least 10 different books, articles or other reference materials. (Your teacher or subject may demand more.) And you should plan on writing two or three drafts of your paper before you arrive at the final copy.

Week 1:	Decide on topic and "angle" of your paper.
Week 2:	Make list of references.
Weeks 3/4:	Read reference materials; take notes.
Weeks 5/6:	Do detailed outline; write first draft.
Week 7:	Edit paper; prepare bibliography.
Week 8:	Proofread paper; type final copy.

Refer to your work schedule often, and adjust your speed if you find yourself lagging behind.

Step 1: Choose your topic

In some cases, your teacher will assign your topic. In others, your teacher will assign a general area of study, but you will have the freedom to pick a specific topic within that general area.

But there are some pitfalls you must avoid. Let's say you need to write a 15-page paper for your American history class. And you decide your topic will be "America's Role in World War II." Can you really cover that in *15* pages? Not unless you simply rehash the high points, *à la* your third-grade history book. You could write *volumes* on the subject (many people have!) and have plenty left to say.

Instead, you need to focus on a particular, limited angle of your subject, such as, "The Role of the Women Air Force Service Pilots in World War II."

How to Study

By the same token, you must not get too narrow in your focus. Choose a subject that's too limited, and you might run out of things to say on the second page of your paper. "The Design of the Women Air Force Service Pilots' Insignia" might make an interesting one- or two-page story. It won't fill 10 or 15 pages.

Pick a topic that's too obscure, and you may find that little or no information has been written about it. In which case, you will have to conduct your own experiments... interview your own research subjects...and come up with your own, original data. (Take it from someone who's done this more than once—it may be wonderfully creative and a lot of fun to work in such original areas, but it can also be frustrating and stressful. And don't underestimate the reaction of your teacher, who may well wish for something a little easier to grade than some far-reaching new theory he or she really needs to think about. I got a "C" on the best paper I think I ever wrote. The grad student grading it came right out and told me since he couldn't "check" my ideas—there was nothing published to support my interpretation—he couldn't give me a better grade. I think that attitude is absurd—and that the "C" was, too—but suggest you keep it in mind.)

Taking all of the above into consideration, do a little brainstorming now about possible topics for your paper. Don't stop with the first idea—come up with several different possibilities. Put this book down until you have a list of three or four potential topics.

Step 2: Begin initial library research

Got your list? Then get thee to a library. You need to do a little advance research. Scan your library's card-catalog index and **Readers' Guide to Periodical Literature** or other publication indexes. See how many books and articles have been written about each topic on your "possibilities" list. Next, read a short background article or encyclopedia entry about each topic.

With any luck at all, you should be left with at least one topic that looks like a good research subject. If two or more topics passed your preliminary-research test, pick the one that interests you most. You're going to spend a lot of time learning about your subject. There's no rule that says you can't enjoy it!

Develop a temporary thesis

Once you have chosen the topic for your paper, you must develop a temporary thesis. (The word "thesis" is a relative of "hypothesis" and means about the same thing—the central argument you will attempt to prove or disprove in your paper.)

A "thesis statement" is a one-sentence summary of your thesis. It sums up the main point of your paper.

Note that I said *temporary* thesis. It may not wind up being your final thesis. Because you haven't completed all your research yet, you can only come up with a "best-guess" thesis at this point.

Some teachers require that you submit your thesis statement for their approval. Even if this is not required, getting your instructor's opinion is always a good idea. Your teacher will be able to help you determine whether your thesis argument is on target.

Step 3: Create a temporary outline

Once you have developed your temporary thesis, give some thought as to how you might approach the subject in your paper. Jot down the various issues you plan to investigate. Then, come up with a brief, temporary outline of your paper, showing the order in which you might discuss those issues.

Don't worry too much about this outline—it will be brief, at best. It's simply a starting point for your research, a plan of attack. But don't skip this step, either—it will be a big help in organizing your research findings.

How to Study

Step 4: Do detailed library research

We've already reviewed the library and how to take advantage of its resources. Now, let's talk about exactly how you'll keep track of all the resources and information you'll gather for your paper.

To create your working bibliography, you'll need a supply of 3 x 5 index cards. You'll also use index cards when you take notes for your paper, so buy a big batch now. About 300 cards ought to suffice.

While you're stocking up on index cards, pick up one of those little envelope files designed to hold the cards. Put your name, address and phone number on the file. If you lose it, some kind stranger can return it.

Start a systematic search for any materials that might have information related to your paper. Look through the indexes we covered in Chapter 6 and any other indexes your librarian recommends.

When you find a book, article or other resource that looks promising, take out a blank note card. On the front of the card, write down the following information:

In the upper right-hand corner of the card: The library call number (Dewey decimal number or Library of Congress number), if there is one. Add any other detail that will help you locate the material on the library shelves (e.g. "Science Reading Room," "Reference Room," "Microfiche Periodicals Room").

On the main part of the card: The author's name, if given—last name first, first name, middle name/initial.

Then the title of the article, if applicable, in quotation marks.

Then the name of the book, magazine, newspaper or other publication—underlined.

Add any details you will need if you have to find the book or article again—date of publication, edition, volume number and page numbers on which the article or information appears.

In the upper left-hand corner of the card: Number it. The first card you write will be #1, the second, #2, and so on. If you happen to mess up and skip a number somewhere along the line, don't worry. It's only important that you assign a different number to each card.

At the bottom of the card: If you're going to be working in more than one library, write the name of the library. Also write down the name of the index in which you found the resource, in case you need to refer to it again.

Do this for *each* potential source of information you find. ***And put only one resource on each card.***

Sample Bibliography Card For A Book

```
(1)                            315.6
                         Main Reading Room

         Jones, Karen A.

     The Life and Times of Bob Smith.
            (see esp. pp. 43-48)

              Card Catalog
            Main Street Library
```

Sample Bibliography Card For A Magazine Article

```
(2)                    Periodical Room

              Perkins, Stan
     "The Life and Times of Bob Smith"
            Smith Magazine
         (April 24, 1989; pp. 22-26)

              Readers' Guide
              University Library
```

Sample Bibliography Card For A Newspaper Article

```
(3)                    Microfiche Room

              Black, Bill
     "Bob Smith: The New Widget Spinner"
            New York Times
    (June 16, 1976, late edition, p. A12)

            New York Times Index
            Main Street Library
```

Now hit the books

Set aside solid blocks of time for your library work. It's better to schedule a handful of extended trips to the library than

15 or 20 brief visits. When you go to the library, take your bibliography cards, a good supply of blank index cards, your preliminary outline and several pens or pencils.

Your bibliography cards are the map for your information treasure hunt. Get out a stack of five or six cards, and locate the materials listed on those cards. Set up camp at a secluded desk or table, and get to work.

A better note-taking system

As I said, when you write your paper, you'll get all the information you need from your notes, rather than from the original sources. Therefore, it's vital that you take careful and complete notes. What sort of information should you put in your notes? Anything related to your subject and especially to your thesis. This includes:

1. General background information—names, dates, historical data, etc.
2. Research statistics
3. Quotes by experts
4. Definitions of technical terms

You may be used to keeping your notes in a three-ring binder or notepad. I'm going to show you a better way—recording all of your notes on index cards.

As was the case with your bibliography cards, you must follow some specific guidelines in order for this system to work. You'll want to refer to the guidelines in this chapter often during your first few note-taking sessions. After that, the system will become second nature to you.

Complete your bibliography card

Let's say that you have found a reference book that contains some information about your subject. Before you begin taking notes, get out the bibliography card for that book.

How to Study

First, check that all of the information on your card is correct. Is the title exactly as printed on the book? Is the author's name spelled correctly?

Next, add any other information you will need to include in your final bibliography. The type of information you need to put on your bibliography card depends on the type of reference material and the bibliography format you are required to use.

Different authorities have put forth different bibliography rules. Be sure to ask your instructor which rules you are to follow! (For more information on exactly what you need to include, be sure to refer to *Write Papers*, one of the six companion books to *How to Study*. It includes details on bibliographic and source note formats.)

Note-taking guidelines

Once your bibliography card is finished, set it aside. Get out some blank index cards, and start taking notes from your reference source. Follow these guidelines:

- *Write one thought, idea, quote or fact on each card.* If you encounter a very long quote or string of data, you can write on both the front and back of a card, if necessary. *But never carry over a note to a second card*.

    What if you simply *can't* fit the piece of information on one card? You're dealing with too much information at once. Break it down into two or more smaller pieces, then put each on a separate card.

- *Write in your own words.* Summarize key points about a paragraph or section. Or restate the material in your own words. Avoid copying things word for word.

- *Put quotation marks around any material copied verbatim.* It's okay to include in your paper a sentence or paragraph written by someone else to emphasize a particular point (providing you do so on a limited basis). But you must copy such statements *exactly as written* in the original—every word, every comma, every period. You also should put each such quote within quotation marks.

Adding detail to your note cards

As you finish each note card, do the following:

- *In the upper left-hand corner of the card:* Write down the resource number of the corresponding bibliography card (in its left-hand corner). This will remind you where you got the information.

- *Below the resource number:* Write down the page(s) on which the information appeared.

- Get out your preliminary outline. Under which outline topic heading does the information on your note card seem to fit? Under your "A" heading? Under "C?" *Jot the appropriate topic letter in the upper right-hand corner of your note card.*

  If you're not sure where the information fits into your outline, put an asterisk (*) instead of a topic letter. Later, when you do a more detailed outline, you can try to fit these "miscellaneous" note cards into specific areas.

- *Next to the topic letter:* Jot down a one- or two-word "headline" that describes the information on the card.

- *When you have finished taking notes from a particular resource,* put a check mark on the bibliography card. This will let you know that you're done with that resource.

How to Study

Be sure that you transfer information accurately to your note cards. Double-check names, dates and other statistics. As with your bibliography cards, it's not so important that you put each of these elements in the places I've outlined above. You just need to be consistent. Always put the page number in the same place, in the same manner. Ditto with the resource number, the topic heading and the headline.

Sample Completed Note Card

(2)   C
p. 22   Education—Degrees
Smith awarded honorary degrees in law from both Harvard & Princeton

Add your personal notes

Throughout your note-taking process, you may want to make some "personal" note cards. On these cards, jot down any thoughts, ideas or impressions you may have about your subject or your thesis.

Perhaps you've thought of a great introduction for your paper. Put it on a card. Or maybe you've thought of a personal experience that relates to your topic. Put it on a card.

Write each thought on a separate note card, as you have with information you've taken from other resources. And assign your note card a topic heading and mini-headline, too. In the space where you would normally put the number of the resource, put your own initials. This will tell you later that "you" were the source of the information or thought.

Step 5: Prepare a detailed outline

It's time to organize your data. You need to decide if your temporary thesis is still on target. You need to determine how you will organize your paper. And you need to create a detailed outline.

Sort your note cards

Once you have your final thesis, begin thinking about how you will organize your paper. This is where the note-card system really pays off. Your note cards give you a great tool for organizing your paper. Get out all of your note cards. Then:

1. Group together all of the cards that share the same outline topic letter (the letter in the right-hand corner of your note card).

2. Put those different groups in order, according to your temporary outline. (Put all of your topic "A" cards at the front of the stack of cards, followed by topic "B" cards, then topic "C" cards, etc.)

3. Within each topic group, sort the cards further. Put together all of the cards that share the same "headline" (the two-word title in the upper-right hand corner of the note card).

4. Go through your miscellaneous topic cards, the ones you marked with an asterisk. Can you fit any of them into your existing topic groups? If you can, re-place the asterisk with the topic letter. If you can't, put the card at the very back of your stack of cards.

Your note cards now should be organized according to your preliminary outline. Take a few minutes to read through your note cards, beginning at the front of the stack and moving through to the back. What you're reading is actually a sketchy draft of your paper—the information you've collected in the order you plan to present it in your paper. Does that order make sense? Or would another arrangement work better?

If necessary, revise your general outline according to the organizational decision you just made. However, don't change the letters that you have assigned to the topics in your outline. (If you decide to put topic B first in your new outline, keep using the letter B in front of it.) Otherwise, the topic letters on your note cards won't jibe with your outline.

Next, go through each group of cards that share the same topic letter. Rearrange them so that they, too, follow the organizational pattern you chose.

After you sort all the cards that have been assigned a specific topic heading (A, B, C, etc.), review cards that are marked with an asterisk. Try to figure out where they fit in your stack of cards.

Your detailed outline is done!

Flip through your note cards from front to back. See that? You've created a detailed outline without even knowing it. The topic letters on your note cards match the main topics of your outline. And those headlines on your note cards? They're the subtopics for your outline.

Simply transfer your note-card headlines to paper. They appear on your outline in the same order as they appear in your stack of cards.

Some instructors require that you get your outline approved before going ahead with your paper. If you have to do this, find out the specific outline format you are to follow. You may need to use a specific numbering/lettering format, such as Roman numerals instead of capital letters for topic headings.

An example of a detailed outline for a paper on women pilots in World War II is on the next page.

Sample Detailed Outline

The Women's Air Force Service in World War II

A. Why civilian women pilots entered the war effort
   1. Shortage of male pilots
   2. Women pilot proposal
   3. Test program begun

B. The type and number of women who participated
   1. Statistics on number of initial participants
   2. Background information about leaders of the program
   3. Participants' socio-economic background

C. Their qualifications and training
   1. Experience needed to be accepted into the program
   2. Training program
      a. ground school
      b. flight school

D. Their missions and contributions
   1. Ferrying planes
   2. Towing targets
   3. Testing repaired planes
   4. Success vs. male pilots

E. The military vs. civilian status question
   1. Reason for initial civilian status
   2. Plan to militarize
   3. Why plan was needed
   4. Why plan was not carried out

F. The disbanding of the group
  1. Additional pilots no longer needed
  2. Male pilots wanted jobs taken over by women
  3. Support for/against disbanding
G. The fight to be recognized as veterans
  1. Importance of the fight
    a. veterans' benefits for the women
    b. recognition of the group's contributions
  2. Instrumental women in the fight
  3. Debate and vote in Congress
  4. Outcome and effect of vote

Step 6: Write the first draft

Actually, you'll find this step easier than you might anticipate. That's assuming that you've done everything as instructed so far—taken good notes, organized your note cards, prepared a detailed outline, etc.

Good writing takes concentration and thought. And concentration and thought require quiet—and lots of it! You also need to have plenty of desk space, so you can spread out your note cards in front of you. Your work area should be well-lit. And you should have a dictionary and thesaurus close at hand.

If possible, work on a computer, so that you can add, delete and rearrange your words easily.

Remember: At this point, your goal is to produce a rough draft—with the emphasis on *rough*. Your first draft isn't supposed to be perfect. It's *supposed* to need revision.

Your thoughts are the foundation of your paper. And you should build the foundation before you worry about the trimmings. So, for now, concentrate just on getting your thoughts on paper. Don't worry about using exactly the right word.

Don't worry about getting commas in all the right places. We'll take care of all that later.

Do a note-card draft

Your note cards helped you come up with a detailed outline. Now, they're going to help you plot out the actual paragraphs and even sentences of your paper.

1. Your note cards should be arranged in the same order as your detailed outline. Take out all of the note cards labeled with the letter of the first topic on your outline.
2. Out of that stack, take out all the cards marked with the same "headline" as the first subheading in your outline.
3. Look at the information on those cards. Think about how the various pieces of information might fit together in a paragraph.
4. Rearrange those cards so they fall in the order you have determined is best for the paragraph.
5. Do this for each group of cards, until you reach the end of the deck.

Now put it all on paper

Take the plunge now, and turn your note-card draft into a written rough draft. Using your cards as your guide, sit down and write.

Double- or triple-space your draft, so that it will be easy to edit later on. After you are finished with a note card, put a check mark at the bottom of the card.

If you decide that you won't include information from a particular card, don't throw the card away...yet. Keep it in a separate stack. You may decide to fit in that piece of information in another part of your paper. Or you may change your mind after you read your rough draft and decide to include the information as planned after all.

How to Study

Help for when you get stuck

Got writer's block already? Here are a few tricks to get you unstuck.

- Pretend you're writing a letter to a good friend, and tell him or her everything you have learned about your subject and why you believe your thesis is correct.
- Use everyday language. Too many people get so hung up on using fancy words and phrases that they forget that their goal is communication. Simpler is better. Drop the "dollar" words and settle for the twenty-five centers.
- Type *something*. Once you have written that first sentence—even if it's a really *bad* first sentence— your brain will start to generate spontaneous ideas.
- Don't edit yourself! As you write your rough draft, don't keep beating yourself up with negatives. Remember, your goal is a *rough* draft.
- Keep moving. If you get hung up in a particular section, don't sit there stewing over it for hours...or even very many minutes. Just write a quick note about what you plan to cover in that section, and go on.
- If you can't get even that much out, skip the section altogether and come back to it later. The point is, do whatever you have to do to keep moving forward. Force yourself to make it all the way through your paper, with as few stops as possible.

Document your sources

To avoid plagiarism, you must document the source when you put any of the following in your paper:

- Quotations taken from a published source
- Someone else's theories or ideas

- Someone else's sentences, phrases or special expressions
- Facts, figures and research data compiled by someone else
- Graphs, pictures and charts designed by someone else

There are some exceptions. You don't need to document the source of a fact, theory or expression that is common knowledge. And you don't need a source note when you use a phrase or expression for which there is no known author.

Footnotes

For many years, the preferred way to credit sources was the footnote. Two other forms of documentation, endnotes and parenthetical notes, are popular now as well.

A footnote is a source note that appears at the bottom of a page of text. You put a raised (superscript) number at the end of the statement or fact you need to document, which tells your readers to look at the bottom of the page for a note about the source of the data.

What goes in a footnote? The same information that's in the bibliography listing. *And* the exact page number the information appears on.

In front of that source note, you put the same superscript number as you put next to the statement or fact in your text.

There is no limit to the number of footnotes you may have in your paper. Number each footnote consecutively, starting with the number 1. For every footnote "flag" in your paper, be sure there is a corresponding source note at the bottom of the page.

Different strokes

Like bibliography listings, different authorities cite different rules for setting up footnotes. Ask your teacher whose rules you are to follow. If your teacher doesn't have a preference, you might as well use the Modern Language Association of America (MLA) rules, which I do. Also, be sure to refer to **Write Papers** for a more in-depth examination of source documentation.

Using the hypothetical paper below, I've included some sample footnotes, based on MLA guidelines, for a book, a magazine article and a newspaper article.

Bob Smith was a leader in the history of Smiths in America. He earned $1 million by the time he was 18.[1] He was awarded honorary degrees in law from Harvard and Princeton.[2] At the age of 35, he invented the first successful widget-spinning gadget,[3] which gave manufacturers a new way to produce widgets.

More than a savvy businessman and accomplished scholar, Smith was a devoted family man. A close friend and neighbor, Bill Jones, once said of Smith: "I never met a man who spent so much time attending to the needs of his wife and children."[4]

[1] Karen A. Jones, The Life and Times of Bob Smith (New York: Smith Press, 1989) 24.

[2] Stan Perkins, "The Life and Times of Bob Smith," Smith Magazine 24 Apr. 1989: 22.

[3] Bill Black, "Bob Smith: The New Widget Spinner," The New York Times 16 June 1976, late ed.: A12.

[4] Jones 38.

Step 7: Do additional research

Did you discover any gaps in your research as you put together your first draft? Raise some questions that you need additional information to answer? Then now's the time to head for the library for one last crack at the books.

Step 8: Write the second draft

The goal for this phase is to edit for meaning—to improve the flow of your paper, organize your thoughts better, clarify confusing points and strengthen any weak arguments.

At this stage, you will focus on all of those problem areas you found. Add new data or information, if need be. Play with sentences, paragraphs and even entire sections. If you're working with a computer, this is fairly easy to do. You can flip words, cut and add sentences, rearrange whole pages with a few keystrokes.

If you're working with a typewriter or pencil and paper, you can do the same thing, but with scissors and tape. Just cut up the pages of your rough draft and tape them together in their new order.

After you've fixed major problem areas, take an even closer look at your sentences and paragraphs. Try to make them smoother, tighter, easier to understand:

- Is there too much fat? Seize every opportunity to say it in fewer words.
- Are there places where phrasing or construction is awkward? Rearrange your words so they "flow" better.
- Did you use descriptive, colorful words? Did you simply tell your reader, "The last days of the war were hard?" Or did you inform them that "the war dragged on, for days...weeks...months, as weary soldiers slogged from battle to bloody battle."

    Consult your thesaurus for synonyms that might do a better job than the words you originally chose. But don't get carried away and use words so obscure that the average reader wouldn't know their meaning. Or that fall on the reader's ear with a "we-don't-really-belong-here-but-*aren't*-we-impressive?" clang.

When in doubt, opt for the familiar word rather than the obscure, the shorter vs. the longer, the tangible vs. the hypothetical, the direct word vs. the roundabout phrase.

- Have you overused particular words? Constantly relying on the same verb or adjective makes your writing boring. Again, check your thesaurus.

- How do the words *sound?* When you read your paper aloud, does it flow like a wonderfully rhythmic piece of music? Or just grind along like a dull dirge? Vary the length of your sentences and paragraphs to make your writing more exciting.

- Always remember the point of the paper—to communicate your ideas as clearly and concisely as possible. So don't get lost in the details. Yes, we've all heard of one famous writer or another who filled a wastebasket with discarded pages before he got one page of usable prose. Whose every word seems to be drawn screaming and kicking from her belly. Hey, this isn't *War and Peace* you're writing here. Relax. If you have to choose between that "perfect" word and the most organized paper imaginable, opt for the latter.

Again, mark corrections on your draft with a colored pen or pencil. No need to retype your paper yet—unless it's gotten so marked up that it's hard to read.

When you finish editing for content and meaning, print or type out a clean copy of your paper.

Step 9: Check spelling and proofread

All right, here's the part that almost nobody enjoys: It's time to rid your paper of mistakes in grammar and spelling.

I know that I've told you your thoughts are the most important element of your paper. It's true. But it's also true that glaring mistakes in grammar and spelling will lead your teacher to believe that you are either careless or downright ignorant. Neither of which will bode well for your final grade.

So, get out your dictionary and a reference book on English usage and grammar. Scour your paper, sentence by sentence, marking corrections with your colored pen or pencil. Look for:

- *Misspelled words.* Check every word. Ask yourself, "If I had to bet $100 that I spelled that word correctly, would I take the bet?" No? Then you'd better look it up in the dictionary. If you're using a spell-checking computer program, be careful of sound-alike words. "There" might be spelled correctly, but not if you meant to write "their".

- *Incorrect punctuation.* Review the rules for placement of commas, quotation marks, periods, etc. Make sure that you follow those rules throughout your paper.

- *Incorrect sentence structure.* Look for dangling participles, split infinitives, sentences that end in prepositions and other no-no's. Again, review the rules about such matters in your reference book.

Step 10: Have someone *else* proofread

Retype your paper, making all those corrections you marked during the last step. Format the paper according to the teacher's instructions. Incorporate your final footnotes and bibliography.

Give your paper a title, if you haven't already done so. Your title should be as short and sweet as possible, but tell readers what they can expect to learn from your paper.

Find someone who is a good proofreader—a parent, relative, friend—and ask him or her to proofread your paper before you put together the final draft.

Steps 11 and 12: The final draft

Incorporate any changes or errors your proofreader may have caught. Type the final draft.

Proof it again—very carefully.

When everything's absolutely perfect, head right for the copy shop. Pay the buck or two it costs to make a copy of your paper. After all your hard work, you want to be sure you have a backup copy in case you lose or damage your original.

Last step? Put your paper in a new manuscript binder or folder. Then, turn it in—on time, of course!

Oral reports

There are some key differences between writing a report and presenting it orally, especially if you don't want to make the mistake of just reading your report in front of the class.

Good notes are your lifeline when you stand up to say what's on your mind. They should act as cues to remind you where your talk should go next, and they should make you feel secure that you can get through the ordeal.

However, notes can also be a crutch that guarantees not success, but audience boredom. You've probably seen any number of people get up in front of an audience and just read some papers they have in front of them.

Is there any *better* cure for insomnia?

As you gather information for your report, making notes on index cards as you did for your term paper, keep this in mind: In order for you to be effective, you must use some different techniques when you *tell* your story rather than *write* it. Here are a few:

- ***Don't make your topic too broad.*** This advice, offered for preparing written reports as well, is even more important when preparing a talk. Try giving an effective speech on "Drugs," "Hamlet" or "Capital Punishment"...in 15 minutes, frequently the amount of time assigned for oral reports. These topics are more suited to a series of books!

"How Shakespeare portrays Hamlet As The Mad Prince" or "Why Drugs Should (or Shouldn't) Be Legalized" or "Why Capital Punishment Is No Deterrent" are more manageable. Narrowing the scope of your talk will help you research and organize it more effectively.

- *Don't overuse statistics.* While they're very important for lending credibility to your position, too many will only weigh down your speech and bore your audience—as anyone who sat through one of the last presidential debates can tell you.

- *Anecdotes add color and life to your talk.* But use them sparingly, because they can slow down your speech. Make sure you get to the punch-line before the yawns start.

- *Be careful with quotes.* Unlike a term paper, a speech allows you to establish yourself as an authority with less fear of being accused of plagiarism. So you can present a lot more facts without attribution. (But you'd better have the sources in case you're asked about your facts.) You can use quotes, though, when they contain distinctive language or elicit an emotion. Be sure to attribute the source.

I've found that trying to shuffle a bunch of papers in front of a class is difficult and that note cards that fit in the palm of your hand are a lot easier to use. But only if the notes on them are very short and to the point, to act as "triggers" rather than verbatim cue cards—hanging on to 300 note cards is as difficult as a sheaf of papers.

How to Study

Remember: You'll actually be holding these cards in your sweaty palms and speaking from them, so write *notes,* not whole sentences. The shorter the notes—and the more often you practice your report so each note triggers the right information—the more effective your report will be. (And the less you will have to look at them, making eye contact with your class and teacher easier.)

As far as ways to make your oral reports more effective, we've already talked about some in Chapter 5, but here are a few more:

- Pick out one person to talk to—preferably a friend, but an animated and/or interested person will do—and direct your talk to him or her.

- Practice, *practice,* **practice** your presentation. Jangled nerves are often the result of a lack of confidence. The more confident you are that you know your material, the less nervous you will be. And the better and more spontaneous your presentation will be.

- If you are like me and suffer from involuntary "shakes" at the mere thought of standing in front of a roomful of people, make sure you can use a lectern, desk or something to cling to.

- Take a deep breath before you go to the front of the class. And don't worry about pausing, even taking another deep breath or two, if you lose your place or find your confidence slipping away.

- If every trick in the world still doesn't steady you down, consider taking a public speaking course (Dale Carnegie, *et al),* joining the Toastmasters Club or seeking out similar extracurricular help.

I've begun to think of my notes for speeches as the purest form of the note-taking craft we've described in this book. You are distilling ideas down to a phrase, a word, a number, perhaps just a symbol that will help you remember under pressure.

Often, the very *process* of taking notes is enough, in and of itself, to ensure that a fact, an impression or a formula will last in your memory for a long time. Note-taking is stripping data down to their essence.

Chapter Eight

HOW TO STUDY FOR TESTS

Quizzes. Midterms. Finals. PSAT. ACT. SAT-I. SAT-II. GMAT. GRE. LSAT. Civil Service exams. Aptitude tests. Employment tests.

Throughout your educational life—and more than likely, the *rest* of your life—testing will be an inevitable if sometimes frightening and distressing reality. So the sooner you learn the techniques of preparing for, taking and mastering tests, the better off you'll be.

What do they want to know?

Many tests are as much a measure of the *way* you study—your ability to organize a mountain of material—as the material itself. This is especially true of any test that purports to measure knowledge spread across the years and your mastery of such a broad spectrum of material—the SATs; GRE; bar or medical exams; exams for nurses, CPAs, financial planners, etc.; or the three days of oral exams my *alma mater* put everyone through. Which means the better you *study*, the better your *score* will probably be on such tests.

There are, as we've already seen, ways to organize your studying to achieve maximum results in minimal time. There are a great number of such techniques to use when studying for tests...of any kind.

Before you can decide how to study for a particular test, it's imperative that you know exactly what you're being tested *on*. Preparing for a weekly quiz is far different than preparing for a final exam. And the biggest final of your life is child's play compared to "monster tests" like the oral exams I faced before they allowed me to graduate college—which covered everything I was supposed to have learned in four years.

Studying for a standardized test like the SAT I, ACT or GRE is also completely different—you can't pull out your textbook and, knowing what chapters are being included, just "bone up."

The structure of the test is also of paramount importance, not necessarily in terms of how you study, but how you tackle it once you get your test book.

What are you afraid of?

Tests are scary creatures. So before I start meting out test-taking techniques, let's tackle one of the key problems many of you will face—test anxiety, that all-too-common reaction to tests characterized by sweaty palms, a blank mind and the insane urge to flee to Pago Pago on the next cargo ship.

What does it mean when someone proclaims they don't "test well"? For many, it really means you don't *study* well (or, at the very least, *prepare* well). For others, it could mean they are easily distracted, unprepared for the type of test they are confronting, or simply unprepared mentally to take *any* test (which may well include mentally sabotaging yourself into a poor score or grade, even though you know the material...backwards and forwards).

Take heart—very few people look forward to a test; more of you are afraid of tests than you'd think. But that doesn't mean you *have* to fear them.

Since we all recognize the competitive nature of tests, being in the right frame of mind when taking them is important. Some of us rise to the occasion when facing such a challenge. Others are thrown off-balance by the pressure. Both reactions probably have little to do with one's level of knowledge, relative intelligence or amount of preparation. The smartest kids in your class may be the ones most afraid of tests.

Generally speaking, the best way to avoid the pitfalls of the extraordinary pressures of a testing situation is to place yourself in that environment as often as possible. Yep. Practice helps.

But there are some other, surprisingly simple steps you can take to give yourself an edge by being less *on* edge.

Dealing with test anxiety

Few people enter a testing site cool, calm and ready for action. Most of us have various butterflies gamboling in our stomachs, sweat glands operating in overdrive and a sincere desire to be somewhere else...*anywhere* else.

Even if you're just entering high school, you have a few years of tests under your belt and should have some idea of how well or poorly you react to a testing situation. If the answer is "not well," start trying some of the following options until you find the one(s) that work for you.

"I know I can, I know I can"

The more pressure you put on yourself—the larger you allow a test (and, of course, your hoped-for good scores) to loom in your own mind—the less you are helping yourself. And, of course, the bigger the test really *is,* the more likely you are to keep reminding yourself of its importance.

No matter how important a test really may be to your career—and, your scores on some *can* have a major effect on where you go to college, whether you go on to graduate school or whether you get the job you want—it is just as important to *de-emphasize* that test's importance in your mind. This should have no effect on your preparation. You should still study as if your life depended on a superior score. It might!

Keeping the whole experience in perspective might also help: Twenty years from now, nobody will remember, or care, what you scored on *any* test—no matter how life-threatening or life-determining you feel that test is right now.

And don't underestimate that old standby, positive thinking: Thoughts *can* become self-fulfilling prophecies. Tell yourself often enough "be careful, you'll fall over that step," and you probably will. Tell yourself often enough "I'm going to fail this test" and you just might. Likewise, keep convincing yourself that you are as prepared as anyone and are going to "ace" the sucker, and you are already ahead of the game.

Hit the road, Jack

You've already found that scheduling breaks during your study routine makes it easier for you to focus on your books and complete your assignments faster and with more concentration. Scheduling breaks during tests has the same effect.

During a one-hour test, you may not have time to go out for a stroll. But during a two- or three-hour final, a major test like the SAT, etc., there's no reason you should not schedule one, two or even more breaks on a periodic basis—whenever you feel you need them most. Such time-outs can consist of a bathroom stop, a quick walk up and down the hall, or just a minute of relaxation in your seat before you continue the test.

How to Study

No matter what the time limits or pressures, don't feel you cannot afford such a brief respite. You may need it *most* when you're convinced you can *least* afford it, just as those who most need time management techniques "just don't have the time" to learn them.

I'm relaxing as fast as I can!

If your mind is a jumble of facts and figures, names and dates, you may find it difficult to zero in on the specific details you need to recall, even if you know all the material backwards and forwards. The adrenaline rushing through your system may just make "instant retrieval" impossible.

The simplest relaxation technique is deep breathing. Just lean back in your chair, relax your muscles and take three very deep breaths (count to 10 while you hold each one). For many of you, that's the only relaxing technique you'll ever need.

There are a variety of meditation techniques that may also work for you. Each is based on a similar principle—focusing your mind on one thing to the exclusion of everything else. While you're concentrating on the object of your meditation (even if the object is nothing, a nonsense word or a spot on the wall), your mind can't be thinking about anything else, which allows it to slow down a bit.

The next time you can't focus, try sitting back, taking three deep breaths and concentrating for a minute or two on the word "Mu." When you're done, you should be in a far more relaxed state and ready to tackle any test.

If you feel you need such help, consider learning some sort of meditation technique or even self-hypnosis.

Whatever such technique you feel you need to use, remember an important fact: The more you believe in the technique, the more it will work. Just like your belief that you're going to "ace" that test!

Make like a scout—be prepared!

Some rites of preparation are pertinent to any test, from a weekly quiz to the SAT I and everything in between:

Plan ahead

I'll admit it. When I was a student, even in college, my attention span tended to be bounded by the weekends. Tell me in October that there would be a big test the first week of December and I'd remember, probably, around November 31.

Of such habits are cramming, crib sheets and failing marks made.

The key to avoiding all of these unpleasantries is review. But *regular, periodic review.* The more often you review, the less often you will have to pull all-nighters the week of the test. You already will have stayed on top of the material, written down and asked questions that arose from your reviews and gone over class and textbook notes to make sure you understand everything. Your last-minute review will be relatively leisurely and organized, not feverish and harried.

In Chapter 4, I included a review schedule on our Project Board (see pages 96 and 97). My suggestion is to set up the simplest review schedule possible, but one you will stick to. For example, you might simply review one subject a week until you have reviewed the previous work for each subject. Then start over again. Sunday mornings might be set aside for this process. Or a weeknight that you normally have free.

Alternatively, you can review the previous week's work in *all* subjects *every* week. Some of you may prefer this method; I personally find it a little unwieldy, preferring to concentrate on just one subject and being able to work as long as necessary without worrying about having to "move on."

Later in this chapter I will be talking about the possibility of forming a study group, which might make the review process even easier.

How to Study

Use *two* alarm clocks

Doing poorly on a test is discouraging. Doing poorly on a test you felt ready for is depressing. Missing the test entirely is devastating. It's imperative that you know when and where all tests are scheduled and allow ample time to get to them.

If you're still in high school, getting to a particular test shouldn't be too hard—it will probably be held during your regular class period and in your normal classroom.

But in college, tests may be scheduled at hours different than the normal class period...and at an entirely different site.

Likewise, major out-of-school tests like the SAT I and II may not even be held at your school. In such cases, make sure you allow enough time to drive to, or be driven to, wherever you have to be—especially if no one is sure how to get there!

As soon as you know the time and location of any major test—midterm, final, SAT I, etc.—enter it on your weekly calendar. Whether in high school, college or grad school, most schools set aside a week, two or even more for final exams. This exam period is usually clearly marked in your college handbook, announced in class (usually on the first day), printed on your class syllabus, etc.

Make optional assignments mandatory

Sometimes, in addition to your regular reading and assignments, the teacher will assign "optional" reading at the beginning of a course. These books, articles, etc., may never be discussed in any class—but material from them may well be included on a test, especially a final exam. If you have neglected to add this supplementary reading to your regular weekly assignments calendar, but wish to read it before the test, make sure you allow enough time to buy or find these books. A lot of other students may have also left such reading to the last minute, and you may be unable to find the material you need if you wait too long.

Pens, pencils...a candy bar

Lastly, bring whatever materials you need to the test, from pens and pencils to calculators. I also recommend—especially for a long test like the SAT I or ACT—that you bring along a candy bar, lifesavers, Granola bar or some other "quick-energy" snack to help buck you up when you need to give yourself a figurative "slap in the face."

Although many testing booklets will include room for notes, it may not be sufficient for your purposes. If you are asked to write three, five or even more essay questions, you will want a lot of scratch paper to outline and organize your thoughts before you put pen to paper. Likewise, a particularly complex math test may quickly use up every square inch of margin. So bring along a separate writing tablet or even a stack of scrap paper. There are few situations in which their use won't be allowed.

If you didn't listen before...

Review, *review,* **review.** If you don't follow my advice for periodic review, you must be sure, especially for midterms and finals, to set aside the time to do the review and studying you need in the week or two before the test.

The more material you need to review, the more important it is to clear your schedule. A four-, five- or six-course load covering 20, 40 or more books, lectures and discussions, papers and projects, easily generates hundreds of pages of notes. Reviewing them, understanding them, studying them will require your full-time effort for a week, even two. So make sure all other end-of-term work, especially major projects like papers, are out of the way.

Whether you need to schedule a solid two weeks for a complete review or just two or three days because you have already reviewed most of your course work on a regular basis, make sure you schedule the time you've allocated on your weekly calendar, allowing more time for the subjects in which you are weakest, of course.

Why cramming *doesn't* work

We've all done it at one time or another, with one excuse or another—waited until the last minute and then tried to cram a week's or month's or entire semester's worth of work into a single night or weekend. Did it work for you? I doubt it.

The reality is that cramming works—on one level—for a small minority of students. Somehow, they're able to shove more "stuff" into short-term memory than the rest of us and actually remember it, at least for 24 hours. After 24 hours? Gone with the wind. Which means if they managed to do well on a weekly quiz, all that cramming didn't do them a bit of good for the midterm or final coming up. And it certainly didn't manage to affect at all what they actually learned from the course, or what they can carry with them, in understanding and knowledge, long after the course is just a memory.

The rest of us don't even get that smidgen of good news—after a night of no sleep and too much coffee, we're lucky if we remember where the test *is* the next morning. A couple of hours later, trying to stay awake long enough to make it back to bed, we haven't even done very well on the test we crammed for!

And that's probably the best reason of all not to cram—it just doesn't work!

How to cram anyway

Nevertheless, despite your resolve, best intentions and firm conviction that cramming is a losing proposition, you may well find yourself in the position of needing to do *some*thing the night before a test you haven't studied for at all. If so, there are some rules to follow that will make your night of cramming at least marginally successful:

Be realistic about what you can do. You absolutely *cannot* master an entire semester's worth of work in a single night, especially if your class attendance has been sporadic (or non-existent) and you've skimmed two books out of a syllabus of two dozen. The *more* information you try to cram in, the *less* effective you will be.

Needless to say, being realistic means a sober assessment of your situation—you're hanging by your thumbs and are just trying to avoid that fall into the boiling oil. Avoiding the oil, saving the damsel in distress and inheriting the kingdom— "acing" the test—is a bit too much to ask for, no matter whom your fairy godmother. And, of course, you are *not* expecting to remember anything about the course after the test, are you?

Be selective and study in depth. The more you've managed to miss, the more selective you need to be in organizing your cram session. You *can't* study it all. Use every technique in this chapter to separate the wheat from the chaff, the important topics from the unimportant (or, at least, the ones you expect to be on the test from the ones you don't). Then study the topics one by one, only moving on to the second when you feel you have an excellent grasp of the first. It really is better in this case to know a lot about a little rather than a little about a lot. Who knows, you may get lucky and pick the three topics the three essays cover!

Massage your memory. Use every memory technique in this book (and the additional ones in ***Improve Your Memory***) to maximize what you're able to retain in your short-term memory. Repetition is key, reciting out loud a good idea.

Know when to give up. When you can't remember your name, give up and get some sleep. Better to arrive at the exam with some sleep under your belt and feeling as relaxed as possible (and *that* means trying to forget that you really didn't study, you crammed, which, if you remembered, would really make you nervous!).

How to Study

Consider an early morning rather than a late-night cram. Especially if you're a "morning" person but even if you're not, I've personally found it more effective to go to bed early and get up early rather than go to bed late and get up exhausted. Such a plan also requires you remembering all this stuff for less time.

Spend the first few minutes writing down whatever you remember now but are afraid you will forget. A suggestion good any time but especially when your mind is trying to retain so many facts and figures it seems ready to explode.

When in doubt, ask

Yes, there are teachers who test you on the most mundane details of their course, requiring you to review every book, every note, every scribble.

I don't think most teachers work that way. You will more than likely be tested on some subset of the course, those particular topics or problems or facts or figures the teacher believes most important.

How do you know what those are? Or, to put it more bluntly, how do you know what's going to be on the test? An important question, especially since I keep urging you to tailor and organize your studying based on such information.

Teachers give many clues. In general, the more often you see or hear the same material, the more important it probably is...and the more likely it will show up on a test. A subhead in your textbook, repeated twice in the same lecture, repeated again just a week before the test? What do you need, a megaphone announcing "This is on the test?!"

A fact or topic need not be repeated in order to scream "Learn Me." Just as you learned to watch a teacher's body language and listen for verbal clues to identify note-worthy topics, you'll learn to identify topics the teacher indicates—nonverbally—are the most important. Your teacher's attitude *toward* note-taking may well tip you off, as well. If he or she requires you to take detailed notes—even wants them turned in (sometimes in high school, never in college)—I'd figure that your class notes are far and away more important than the textbook(s).

Have you saved earlier tests and quizzes from that class? Returned exams, especially if they contain a lot of comments from your teacher, should give you an excellent indication of where to concentrate your study time.

Is it wrong to ask the teacher what kind of test to expect? Absolutely not.

Will he or she always tell you? Absolutely not.

But it is also not wrong to research that teacher's tests from previous years—students a year or two ahead of you can sometimes be of invaluable help in this effort.

Why? Because, like most of us, teachers are creatures of habit. While you certainly shouldn't expect to find questions that will be duplicated, you can glean a few key things from previous tests, like the format the teacher seems to prefer and the areas that seem to be stressed.

Don't take any of this as a "given," however: Even creatures of the most set habits have been known to turn over a new leaf now and then.

More list-making, please

Once you've discovered the type of test facing you, you want to figure out what's actually going to be *on* it (and, hence, what you actually need to study). And, remember, it's rarely, if ever, "everything."

In general, take the time to eliminate from consideration, with the possible exception of a cursory review, material you are convinced is simply not important enough to be included on an upcoming test. This will automatically give you more time to concentrate on those areas you are sure *will* be included.

How to Study

Then create a "To Study" sheet for each test. On it, list specific books to review, notes to recheck, specific topics, principles, ideas and concepts to go over, etc. Then just check off each item as you study it. This is akin to breaking the paper-writing process into thirteen smaller, easier-to-accomplish steps. And it will have the same effect—to minimize procrastination, logically organize your studying and give you ongoing "jolts" of accomplishment as you complete each item.

Test yourself

Just as you have made it a habit to write down questions as you study your texts, why not try to construct your own tests? And remember: The harder you make them, the better prepared and more confident you will be walking into the test.

Practice tests offer some real advantages, whether you're studying for a weekly quiz, the SAT I or your bar exam. In fact, the longer and more "standardized" the test, the more important it is to be familiar with its structure, its rules and its traps.

First and foremost, familiarization with whatever type of test you're taking is vitally important, as it enables you to strategically study the material (prioritize) and strategically attack the test (organize). Familiarization breeds comfort and, as I've pointed out more than once, being comfortable—relaxed—is a key component to doing well.

Familiarization also breeds organization, allowing you to concentrate on the test itself and not on its structure. Which, of course, gives you more time to actually *take* the test rather than figure it out. It also reduces the effect of whatever time restraints the test imposes on you. The greater the time restraints, the more practicing will enable you to deal with them on the actual test, minimizing the pressure.

Last but not least, doing practice tests is a highly effective way to study and remember the material.

Test-day rules and reminders

If the test is not simply during a regular class period, make sure to arrive at the test site early. Based on your preferences (from Chapter 2), sit where you like.

Be careful, however. There may be some variations here you have to take into account. In a test where there are 200 or 300 people in a room, there is a distinct advantage to sitting near the front: You can hear instructions and the answers to questions better. And you generally get the test first.

Know the ground rules

Will you be penalized for guessing? The teacher, for example, may inform you that you will earn two points for every correct answer but *lose* one point for every incorrect one. This will certainly affect whether you guess or skip the question—or, at the very least, how many potential answers you feel you need to eliminate before the odds of guessing are in your favor.

Are the questions or sections weighted? Some tests may have two, three or more sections, some of which count for very little—10 or 20 percent of your final score—while one, usually a major essay, may be more heavily weighted—50 percent or more of your grade. This should drastically alter the time you spend on each section.

Discriminate and eliminate

There is usually nothing wrong with guessing, unless, of course, you know wrong answers will be penalized. Even then, as I've pointed out, guessing is not necessarily wrong. The question is how *much* to guess.

If there is no penalty for wrong answers, you should *never* leave an answer blank. But you should also do everything you can to increase your odds of getting it right. If every multiple-choice question gives you four possible answers, you have a 25-

percent chance of being right (and, of course, a 75-percent chance of being wrong) each time you have to guess.

But if you can eliminate a single answer—one you are reasonably certain cannot be right—your chances of being correct are 33 percent.

And, of course, if you can get down to a choice between two answers, it's just like flipping a coin: 50-50. In the long run, you will guess as many right as wrong.

Even if there is a penalty for guessing, I would probably pick one answer if I had managed to increase my chances of getting the right one to 50-50.

Presuming that you've managed to eliminate one or more answers but are still unsure of the *correct* answer—and have no particular way to eliminate further—here are some real insider tips to make your "guessing" on multiple-choice questions more "educated":

- If two answers are very close in meaning, choose one.
- If two answers sound alike, choose one.
- If the answers to a mathematical question cover a broad range, choose the one in the middle.
- If two quantities are very close, choose one.
- If two numbers differ only by a decimal point (and the others aren't close), choose one of them. (Example: 2.3, 40, 1.5, 6, 15; I'd go for either 1.5 or 15. If I could at least figure out from the question where the decimal point should go, even better!)
- If two answers to a mathematical problem *look* alike—either formulas or shapes—choose one.

What about going back, rechecking your work, and changing a guess? How valid was that first guess? Surprisingly, perhaps, statistics show it was probably pretty darned good (presuming you had some basis for guessing in the first place). So good that you should only change it if:

- It really was just a wild guess and, upon further thought, you conclude that answer really should be eliminated (in which case your next guess is, at least, not quite so wild).

- You remembered something that changes the odds of your guess completely (or the answer to a later question helped you figure out the answer to this one!).

- You miscalculated on a math problem.

- You misread the question (didn't notice a "not", a "never", an "always" or other important qualifier).

Answer every fourth question

Read and understand the directions. As I stressed in Chapter 7, you could seemingly do everything *right*, but not follow your teacher's explicit directions, in which case everything's *wrong*.

If you're supposed to check off *every* correct answer to each question in a multiple choice test—and you're assuming only *one* answer to each question is correct—you're going to miss a lot of answers!

If you're to pick one essay question out of three, or two out of five, that's a lot different than trying to answer every one. You won't do it. And even if you do, the teacher will probably only grade the first two. Because you needed to allocate enough time to do the other three, it's highly doubtful your first two answers will be so detailed and perfect that they will be able to stand alone.

And be aware of time. Again, if questions or sections are weighted, you will want to make sure you allow extra time for those that count the most. Better to do a superior job on the two sections that count for 90 percent of the score and whip through the 10-percent section as the teacher is collecting booklets.

How to Study

I know students who, before they write a single answer, look through the entire test and break it down into time segments— allocating 20 minutes for section one, 40 for section two, etc. Even on multiple choice tests, they count the total number of questions, divide by the time allotted and set "goals" on what time they should reach question 10, question 25, 50, etc.

I never did it. But I think it's a great idea—if it turns out to be a workable organizational tool for you and not just one more layer of pressure.

If there are pertinent facts or formulas you're afraid you'll forget, I also think it's a good idea to write them down somewhere in your test booklet before you do anything else. It won't take much time and it could save you some serious memory jogs later.

First out could be first failed

Leave time at the end of every test to recheck your answers.

And speaking of time, don't make a habit of leaving tests early. There is little to be gained from supposedly "impressing" the teacher and other students with how smart you (think you) are by being first to finish. Take the time to make sure you've done your best. If you are completely satisfied with your answers to all questions, it's fine to leave, even if you are first. But in general, slowing down will help you avoid careless mistakes.

Likewise, don't worry about what everybody else is doing. Even if you're the last person left, who cares? Everybody else could have failed, no matter how early and confidently they strode from the room! So take all the time you need and do the best you can.

Test-taking strategies

In addition to some of the general ideas we've talked about, there are very specific strategies to use depending on the type of test you're taking. Let's look at them one at a time.

All of the above again?

There are three ways to attack a multiple-choice test:

1. Start at the first question and keep going, question by question, until you reach the end, never leaving a question until you have either answered it fully or made an educated guess.
2. Answer every *easy* question—the ones you know the answers to without any thinking at all or those requiring the simplest calculations—first, then go back and do the harder ones.
3. Answer the *hardest* questions first, then go back and do the easy ones.

None of these three options is inherently right or wrong. Each may work for different individuals. (And I'm assuming that these three approaches are all in the context of the test format. Weighted sections may well affect your strategy.)

The first approach is, in one sense, the quickest, in that no time is wasted reading through the whole test trying to pick out either the easiest or hardest questions. Presuming that you do not allow yourself to get stumped by a single question so that you spend an inordinate amount of time on it, it is probably the method most of you employ.

Remember, though, to leave questions that confuse you from the outset to the end and allocate enough time to both go back to those you haven't answered and check *all* your answers thoroughly.

The second approach ensures that you will maximize your right answers—you're marking those you are certain of first.

It may also, presuming that you knock off these easy ones relatively fast, give you the most time to work on those that you find particularly vexing.

Many experts recommend this method because they maintain that answering so many questions one after another gives you immediate confidence to tackle the questions you're not sure about. If you find that you agree, then by all means use this strategy. However, you may consider just *noting* the easy ones as you preread the test. This takes less time and, to me, delivers the same "confidence boost."

The last approach is actually the one I use. In fact, I make it a point to do the very hardest question first, then work my way "down" the difficulty ladder. It may sound like a strange strategy to you, so let me explain the psychology.

First of all, I figure if time pressure starts getting to me at the end of the test, I would rather be in a position to answer the easiest questions—and a lot of them—in the limited time left than ones I really have to think about. After all, by the end of the test, my mind won't be working as well as at the beginning!

And that's a major benefit of the third approach: When I am most "up," most awake, most alert, I am tackling those questions that require the most analysis, thinking, interpretation, etc. When I am most tired—near the end—I am answering the questions that are virtually "gimmes."

At the same time, I am also giving myself a *real* shot of confidence. As soon as I finish the first hard question, I already feel better. When I finish all of the hard ones, everything is downhill.

It is not the approach for everybody, but it may be for you.

I would always, however, try to ensure adequate time to at least put down an answer for every question. Better to get one question wrong and complete three other answers than get one right and leave three blank.

And don't fall into the "answer daze," that blank stare some students get when they just can't think of an answer— for 10 minutes. Do *some*thing. Better to move on and get that one question wrong than waste invaluable time doing nothing.

Here are two other tips specifically for non-mathematical multiple-choice tests:

If you're supposed to read a long passage and then answer questions about it, read the questions *first*. That will tell you what you're looking for and *affect the way you read the passage*. If dates are asked for, circle all dates in the passage as you read. If you're looking for facts rather than conclusions, it will, again, change the way you read the passage.

The longest and/or most complicated answer to a question is often correct—the test maker has been forced to add qualifying clauses or phrases to make that answer complete and unequivocable.

And two other tips for *all* multiple-choice tests:

"All of the above" is often the right answer if it is an option. And *hope* that you see it as a potential answer to *every* question because *it gives you a much better chance to do better on the test* than your mastery of the material (or lack thereof) might normally warrant. You might even get all of the questions right without ever being *really* sure that any of the answers you've chosen are right. Why? Because you don't have to be really sure that "all of the above" is correct to choose it. All you have to be is *pretty* sure that *two* answers are correct (and equally sure the others are not *necessarily* wrong). As long as there is—you feel—more than one correct answer, then "all of the above" must be the right choice!

One trick a friend recently suggested has proved extremely useful: When you first read the question—but before you even look at the answer choices—decide what you think the answer is. If your answer is one of the choices you've been given, bingo!

50/50 odds aren't bad. True or false?

I think true-false tests are generally more insidious than multiple-choice, simply because the latter at least offers you the correct answer, which you may well pick out without even knowing it's correct.

How to Study

That's the bad news.

The good news is that it's hard to beat 50-50 odds!

What can you do to increase your scores on true-false tests?

First of all, be more inclined to guess if you have to. After all, I encouraged you to guess on a multiple-choice test if you could eliminate enough wrong answers to get down to two, one of which is correct. Well, you're already there! So, unless you are being penalized for guessing, guess away! (And even if you are being penalized, you may well want to take a shot if you have the faintest clue of the correct answer.)

What tricks do test makers incorporate in true-false tests? Here are three to watch out for:

Two parts (statements) that *are* true (or, at least, *may* be true) linked in such a way that the *whole* statement becomes false. Example: "Since many birds can fly, they use stones to grind their food." Many birds *do* fly, and birds *do* swallow stones to grind their food. But a *causal relationship* (the word "since") between the two clauses makes the whole statement false.

"The longest and/or most complicated answer to a question is often correct—the test maker has been forced to add qualifying clauses or phrases to make that answer complete and unequivocable." That's what I just told you regarding multiple-choice tests. The exact *opposite* is true regarding true-false tests: The longer and/or more complicated a statement in a true-false test, the *less* likely it's true since *every clause* of it must be true (and there are so many chances for a single part of it to be false).

Few broad, general statements are true *without exception.* So always be on your guard when you see the words "all", "always", "no", "never" or other absolutes. As long as you can think of a *single* example that proves such a statement false, then it is false. But be wary: There are statements with such absolutes that *are* true; they are just rare.

Are you *sure* you want to use your book?

I'm convinced these are the toughest tests of all, if only because even normally "nice" teachers feel no compunction whatsoever about making such tests as tough as a Marine drill instructor. Heck, *you can use your book!* That's like having a legal crib sheet, right? Worse yet, many open-book tests are also take-home tests, meaning you can use your notes (and any other books or tools you can think of).

Since you have to anticipate that there will be *no* easy questions, no matter how well you know the material, you need to do some preparation before you enter the room for this type of test:

- Mark important pages by turning down corners, using paper clips or any other method that will help you quickly flip to important charts, tables, summaries or illustrations.

- Write an index of the pages you've turned down so you know where to turn immediately for a *specific* chart, graph, table, etc.

- Summarize all important facts, formulas, etc. on a separate sheet.

- (If you are also allowed to bring your notes or it's a take-home test), write a brief index to your notes (general topics only) so you know where to find pertinent information.

Answer the questions you don't need the book for first, including those of which you're fairly sure and know where to check the answers in your book. Star these latter ones.

Then use the book. Check your starred answers first and erase the stars once you have checked. Then work on those questions on which you must rely fully on the book.

How to Study

Write on!

While I think open-book tests are the hardest ones given, I must admit I think *all* "objective" tests—including multiple-choice and true-false—are harder than an essay test. Since I suspect many of you don't agree, let me explain: I think an objective test of any kind gives the teacher much more latitude, even the option of focusing *only* on the obscurest details (which, granted, only the truly sadistic would do). As a result, it's much more difficult to eliminate areas or topics when studying for such a test (except, as noted, by using the clues the teacher has given you about the relative importance of certain topics and whatever your research into returned examinations and those from previous years has turned up).

It's also rare to be given a choice—answer any 25 out of 50—whereas you may often be given, for example, five essay questions and have to choose only three. This greatly increases the odds that even sporadic studying will have at least given you some semblance of understanding about one or two of the questions, whereas you may be lost on a 100-question true-false test.

Second, less could go wrong on an essay test—there were only three or four questions to read, not a hundred potential *mis*reads. I could think of a few questions, not hundreds. I could take the time to organize (a strength) and would probably get extra points for good spelling, grammar and writing (another strength). It's also a lot easier to budget time among three or four essay questions than among 150 multiple-choice.

Whether you love or hate essays, there are some important pointers to ensure you a least score better on them.

Approach essay questions the same way you would a paper. While you can't check your textbook or go to the library to do research, the facts, ideas, comparisons, etc. you need are in your own cerebral library—your mind.

Here's the step-by-step way to answer every essay question:

Step One: On a blank sheet of paper, write down all the facts, ideas, concepts, etc. you feel should be included in your answer.

Step Two: Organize them in the order in which they should appear. You don't have to rewrite your notes into a detailed outline—why not just number each note according to where you want to place it?

Step Three: Compose your first paragraph, working on it just as long and as hard as I suggested you do on your papers. It should summarize and introduce the key points you will make in your essay. *This is where superior essay answers are made or unmade.*

Step Four: Write your essay.

Step Five: Reread your essay and, if necessary, add points left out, correct spelling, grammar, etc. Also watch for a careless omission that could cause serious damage, such as leaving out a "not", making the point opposite of the one you wanted to.

If there is a particular fact you know is important and should be included but you just don't remember it, guess if you can. Otherwise, just leave it out and do the best you can. If the rest of your essay is well-thought-out and organized and clearly communicates all the other points that should be included, I doubt most teachers will mark you down too severely for such an omission.

Remember: Few teachers will be impressed by length. A well-organized, well-constructed, specific answer to their question will always get you a better grade than "shotgunning"—writing down everything you know in the faint hope that you will actually hit something.

How to Study

If you don't have the faintest clue what the question means, ask. If you still don't have any idea of the answer—and I mean *zilch*—leave it blank. Writing down everything you think you know about the supposed subject in the hopes that one or two things will actually have something to do with the question is, in my mind, a waste of everyone's time. Better to allocate the time you would waste to other parts of the test and do a better job on those.

What if time runs out?

While you should have carefully allocated sufficient time to complete each essay before you started working on the first, things happen. And you may find yourself with two minutes left and one essay to go. What do you do? As quickly as possible, write down and organize all the facts, ideas and concepts you feel should be included in your answer. If you then have time to reorganize your notes into a better-organized outline, do so. Many teachers will give you at least partial credit (some very near *full* credit) if your outline contains all the information the answer was supposed to. It will at least show you knew a lot about the subject and were capable of outlining a reasonable response.

One of the reasons you may have left yourself with insufficient time to answer one or more questions is because you knew too darned much about the previous question(s). And you wanted to make sure the teacher *knew* you knew, so you wrote...and wrote...and wrote...until you ran out of time. Be careful—some teachers throw in a relatively general question that, if you wanted to, you could write about until next Wednesday. In that case, they aren't testing your knowledge of the whole subject as much as your ability to *edit* yourself, to organize and summarize the *important* points. Just remember that no matter how fantastic your answer to any one essay, it is going to get one-fifth the overall score (presuming five questions)—that is, 20 points, never more, even if you turn in a publishable book manuscript. Meanwhile, 80 points are waiting for you.

As I stressed about writing papers, worry less about the specific words and more about the information. Organize your answer to a fault and write to be understood, not to impress. Better to use shorter sentences, paragraphs and words—and be clear and concise—than to let the teacher fall into a clausal nightmare from which he may never emerge.

Read the instructions and question carefully. If you're supposed to "compare and contrast", don't just compare. If you're to analyze, don't just summarize. And if you're supposed to discuss three key reasons something occurred, don't stop at two! In fact, I would go out of my way to underline each key point in any essay that requires a specific number of ways, reasons, explanations, whatever, to make sure a tired teacher doesn't miss one and mark you down for it.

Standardized tests

The various standardized tests used in college and graduate school admissions—the "new" SAT-I, ACT, LSAT, GRE, etc.—require their own pointers. These, like my oral exams at the end of four years of college, are not specific to any course or even one grade. Rather, they are attempting to assess your ability to apply mathematical concepts, read and understand various passages and demonstrate word skills.

Despite their ephemeral nature, you *can* study for them by practicing. There are a variety of companies specializing in preparing students for each of these tests—your school might even sponsor its own course. And any bookstore will probably have shelves of preparation guides.

Given their importance, I would recommend investing the time and money in any such reputable course—Stanley Kaplan, Princeton Review, BAR/BRI, etc.—or, at the very

How to Study

least, buying one of the major preparation books. (I discuss the use and misuse of both in greater detail in one of **How to Study**'s six companion books—*"Ace" Any Test*—available now in a completely up-to-date second edition).

Because these are, indeed, *standardized* tests, learning and utilizing specific techniques pertinent to them and practicing on tests given previously can significantly increase your scores, if only because you will feel less anxious and have a better idea of what's in store for you.

If you are an avid reader and understand what you read, do well in school in most subjects (but especially English and math), and "test well," you may not feel you need such help. That's okay, too. But do note that many of the questions on these tests are word-related—"SWAN is to DUCK as YOGURT is to _____"—testing both your basic vocabulary and your specific understanding of synonyms (words with similar meanings) and antonyms (words with opposite meanings).

So if you don't decide to take one of the review courses, you might still consider getting a good vocabulary book—*Increase Your Word Power in 30 Days* or something similar—as a study aid for such tests.

There are students who achieve exceptional test scores on their SATs and go on to compile barely adequate college records. These people are said to "test well." The testing environment doesn't throw them and they have sufficient prior experience to have a decided edge on the rest of the competition. Others "choke" during such tests but wind up at the top of the career pyramid.

So such testing must be kept in perspective. Though one method of predicting success, such tests are not, by any means, perfect oracles. Nor are their conclusions inalienable. Many people have succeeded in life without ever doing particularly well on achievement tests.

Whether you have traditionally done well or poorly on such tests, I would always recommend minimizing distractions prior to such a big test. Three days before the SAT is *not* the time to dump a girlfriend, move, make a decision about college (especially if you're torn between two or more) or do anything else out of the ordinary. You'll be under enough stress, thank you, without going out of your way to produce more!

What's new about the SAT?

As of March, 1994, students will no longer take the SAT, which stood for the Scholastic Aptitude Test. Now they must prepare for the SAT-I, the Scholastic Assessment Test. The Achievement Tests are also renamed—they are now called the "SAT-II." So what's new in addition to the verbiage and number change?

Contrary to previous reports, *an essay is not part of the regular SAT-I* test. There *is* an essay on the SAT-II Writing Test (which is not required).

Not all questions will be multiple choice. Out of 60 SAT-I math questions, for example, 10 will offer no choices at all. You have to come up with the right answer on your own.

Say good-by to antonyms, which are no longer included. However, the vocabulary used in the sentence completion questions, analogies and reading comprehension selections will be more difficult.

Scoring for each section (verbal and math) still ranges from 200 to 800, but the number of verbal questions counted in your score has been reduced from 85 to 78. Seventy-five minutes is still allotted for that section (and 75 minutes for the 60 math questions, unchanged in number from previous years).

There will still be a 30-minute experimental section in either verbal or math. *These questions and answers don't count in any score.*

How to Study

Say hello to calculators, which can now be brought and used. According to the SAT experts I spoke with, there will *not* be any questions designed to be *easier* to solve with calculators. Indeed, they are designed to be solved just as quickly (and, in some cases, *more* quickly) with*out* a calculator.

Watch those guesses—There is a 1/4 point penalty for an incorrect answer to a question offering five answer choices, a 1/3 point penalty for one offering four choices. Strategize accordingly!

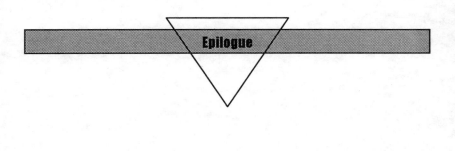

I'm proud of you. You made it all the way through the book. Here's my final advice:

- Reread *How to Study*, cover to cover. It's kind of like seeing a movie for the second time—you always find something you missed the *first* time around.
- Start practicing what I preached. You had an excuse for flunking before—you didn't know how to study. Now you have absolutely *no* excuse for not doing better.
- Buy, read and put into practice whichever of the six companion volumes you need.
- Write me a letter to tell me what helped, how much better you're doing in school or to let me know what else I can include to add to the value of the books. Send your letters to:

> Ron Fry
> c/o Career Press
> P.O. Box 34
> Hawthorne, NJ 07507

I promise I'll try to respond if you ask me to. But please avoid calling me. I'll probably be on the road promoting *How to Study!*

Good studying!

INDEX

How to Study